The Importance of
Failing Well

The Importance of
Failing Well

Lance G King

Chiron Trust for Educational Research

Title: The Importance of Failing Well

Author: Lance G. King

Publisher: The Chiron Trust for Educational Research

Address: 19 Long Street, Raglan 3225

Format: Softcover

Publication Date: 6/2014

ISBN: ISBN 978-0-473-28858-7 (Print)

                  ISBN 978-0-473-29749-7 (Epub)

                  ISBN 978-0-473-29917-0 (Kindle)

First Published in New Zealand in July 2014 by the Chiron Trust for Educational Research.

"Over the last few years Lance King has had a significant influence on the curriculum development of the IB's programmes. First with the IBCC then most recently with the Middle Years Programme and now with the Diploma Programme. His ideas around the development of resilience and the use of learning skills focused, guided inquiry learning in the classroom have been potentially transformative and have helped shape the direction of all of these programmes.

By the time all his present work is released his ideas will be influencing the learning of up to 750,000 students in 3,500 schools in 120 countries."

Malcolm Nicolson, Head of Diploma Programme Development - International Baccalaureate Organization, The Hague

"Mr King and his team are all New Zealanders and they travel the world working with students, teachers and parents delivering their message of the importance of helping children to master good learning skills. The Art of Learning is a programme of learning skills taught in a very interactive and stimulating way. At the end of each course day all the students are energised, motivated and have learned a set of new skills to help them in their academic achievement."

Terry Hedger, Principal, Southbank School, London

"Mr. King presents the necessary skills required in a practical "hands-on" way that allows the students to feel comfortable and to gain confidence. He encourages resilience and self-motivation and presents his ideas with a sense of humour and enthusiasm that shows he is really interested in and convincing about what he says. The student workshops were reinforced by evening presentations to staff and parents not only on the "Art of Learning", but also teaching and living with gifted and talented students. These were overwhelmingly successful and I have heard from both these groups of people that they are incorporating his ideas in their day to day lesson and family planning."

Maggie McCorkell, Principal, Warwick Academy, Bermuda

"The pupils explore and work through a number of skills, which they need to be successful at learning. In that process they raise their self-esteem and confidence and they learn the importance of being resilient. With their multi-sensory teaching styles, their New Zealand stories and their wonderful sense of humour, the Art of Learning presenters reach all pupils. They create a day with a difference. The impact is immediate and amazing. A follow up workshop for staff and a separate workshop for parents complement this programme, thus ensuring that all parties in the "pupil, parent, teacher partnership" are aware of the strategies and the level of support which are required to make learning successful. Parents just love the workshop. At the end of the session, they feel so much better equipped to support their child, not just in terms of practical learning strategies, but also in relation to instilling and boosting their child's confidence."

Ms Lies Goodchild, Head of Learning Support, Kings College School, Wimbledon, London.

Lance's workshops and training are supported by extensive reading and research he has done. He is also happy to share his knowledge, materials and research as well as his time, offering free seminars for parents, websites for schools. I have worked alongside Lance, co-authoring books for the IB, and can only admire his dedication to his work. He is an incredibly hardworking practitioner, highly professional in his approach, and someone who is constantly seeking to further his knowledge and interest in teaching and learning.

Graham Maclure, IB Co-ordinator, Greengates School, Mexico City

"By teaching our most under-achieving boys the skills of effective study and exam preparation, along with self-motivation and resilience building, Mr King's Art of Learning programme has dramatically lifted their performance resulting in record exam results for Harrow School for the last six years – the best in living memory."

Dr Iain W Farrell, Director of Studies, Harrow School, London

"Lance spent the whole day with all of our Year 11 pupils, the majority of whom were second language learners. In the time I spent with Lance and the pupils I saw that they were really interested in what he had to say, as I was myself. Talking to them afterwards their enthusiasm for the course was overwhelming; they were unanimous in their opinions of how useful and interesting it was, but also how much they enjoyed it. Much of this is to do with the friendly and approachable nature of Lance who seems to draw the pupils out of themselves."

John Rolfe, Director of Studies, Shrewsbury International School, Bangkok

We are trying to instil the importance of resilience and independence of learning in our girls. The Art of Learning did not disappoint. Highly experienced presenters tutors came to work with the girls and every feedback form following each conference has been shown to me, evidencing the enormous benefit the girls have received. In addition Lance King, the Director, personally came to train our staff and followed this up with an evening for parents. These were also very well received.
So pleased were we that we extended the programme to Year 10 and the girls regularly refer to some of the techniques they have learnt. In particular the girls have begun to change their mindset and open their minds to the various possibilities for them."

Lorna Duggleby, Head. Bromley High School, Kent, UK

Contents

"Education is a social process. Education is growth. Education is not a preparation for life; education is life itself."

John Dewey

1. Purpose

What do you want from your school?
What do you want your school to do for your children?

I have four children of my own who range from 22 to 30 years old. Two have 'proper jobs' and two are at university. All four now live away from home, the youngest moving out very recently. In their high school years they each performed quite differently and achieved very diverse results. One did brilliantly, obtained the highest possible academic results in New Zealand, one did very well and two dropped out before they finished, one after Year 12 (Grade 11) and one after Year 11 (Grade 10). They are all now doing something that they like doing and feeling successful at it and I am left wondering just how much have their present lives been shaped by their high school experience.

When my children were in high school I was very clear about what I wanted those schools to achieve with them. That was, to prepare each and every one of them to be successful in the adult world once they left school. Simple enough. Much like every parent, I would think. I was expecting the school to inculcate into my children the right skills, knowledge, aptitudes and attitudes to enable them to be competent, skilled, knowledgeable and employable.

But working out exactly what today's teenagers need in order to become successful tomorrow has always been the challenge for school education and never more so than today.

"One's philosophy is not best expressed in words; it's expressed in the choices one makes. In the long run, we shape our lives and we shape ourselves. The process never ends until we die. And the choices we make are ultimately our responsibility."

Eleanor Roosevelt

This challenge I have tried to represent in the symbol of my company – The Art Of Learning.

Centaur

Now this figure is a centaur from Greek mythology and the most famous centaur was a teacher named Chiron. Chiron was the tutor of all the ancient Greek heroes - Jason, Ulysses, Hercules and Achilles, and Chiron was said to be the wisest creature on earth at that time. So I chose the figure of a centaur to represent teachers, who are, of course, the wisest creatures on earth. If the Chiron figure is the teacher then the arrow you can see in the picture represents the student. The teacher's role is to draw back the string on the bow. In other words, to prepare that student thoroughly and completely to be successful in the real world. So that when the arrow leaves the bow, when your children and mine finish school, they leave with everything they need to be a success, to achieve what they want to in the world. And when that arrow is let fly it can fly as far and as fast as possible.

Nice metaphor. But is it realistic? Can we really expect schools to do all that for our children? I think that sometimes as parents we do expect them to, but think for a moment how difficult that task is in the modern world.

In order for schools to be able to prepare someone well for the future they have to have a good idea of what that future will be like and what it will take to be successful in that future.

Once upon a time that was very easy – at least here in New Zealand it was.

For example, my father grew up in the depression years in New Zealand and before he could embark on any chosen career, the Second World War broke out and like all his friends he enlisted in the Army. He served his full term and when the war was over his highest priority was security and so he took accountancy qualifications and a job with the government.

He had a career for life, he worked for 25 years for the same government department, retired at 55 with his war pension and his superannuation and lived a quiet contented life until he died at home at 82. Having experienced both the Depression and the Second World War all either of my parents wanted was a safe, secure, very predictable life in a very predictable world.

"Success is getting what you want. Happiness is wanting what you get."

Dale Carnegie

In my life too things certainly started out very predictably. When I left school in the early '70s in New Zealand there were plenty of jobs for school leavers. Apprenticeships available in all trade areas and there were plenty of places available at university. I had majored in all the sciences at high school and so I went to Massey University to study Food Technology. In my graduating class in 1977, I can still remember our professor coming into class with a list of all the professional positions that were on offer for us, and there were three times as many offers on that list as there were graduates that year! Once again, only 37 years ago it was very easy to predict what skills and knowledge you needed to create a good career for yourself and to create success out there in the real world.

But is that still the case today?

Is it still easy to predict the knowledge and skills, abilities and talents that will be most in demand in our future?

In my life since graduating in '78 as a Food Technologist, I have had six different jobs with four different companies and I have had three complete career changes. I no longer work in the field of my first degree at all, and as an entrepreneur I have suffered complete business failure more than once and have completely re-invented my business on numerous occasions.

And am I happy? Absolutely! I love what I do, I have complete freedom and choice over my life, I travel a lot bringing my ideas to teenagers and their teachers and parents all around the world, I live in a small beach spot in New Zealand that I think is paradise, my wife and family all appear to be happy and thriving and I get time to study and to write. And does my present success have anything at all to do with my schooling? I think so, but not necessarily in a predictable or straight-forward way.

We live in unprecedented times as I'm sure you are aware. How many of you can remember what it was like to live without a cell phone or the internet? Did you know that after radio was invented it took roughly 50 years to reach 50 million people? TV took 20 years to reach the same number, the internet took six years and it took just three minutes for news of Princess Diana's death to circle the globe.

Rapid change is the only thing we can predict with certainty. The challenge for all schools and all parents today is to work out what our children will need in order to be successful in a world that we cannot foresee from where we stand today.

"Knowledge is of two kinds.
We know a subject ourselves,
or we know where we can find
information upon it."

Samuel Johnson

To do this we need to know something about the future. So what do we know for sure? We know something about information. In 1973 a French economist named *Georges Anderla* calculated that if you took the sum total of human knowledge, that is all the information available to humanity at the year:

0		**and called it**		**1 unit**
then it took until the year	**1500**	**to double to**		**2 units**
and then it took until	**1750**	**to double again to**		**4 units**
and until	**1900**	**to double again to**		**8 units**

Notice how quickly the time gap shortens. 1500 years for the first doubling, 250 years for the second, 150 years for the third.

The next complete doubling of all the information available to humanity took until

1950	**and then just until**
1960	**to double again**

Anderla then calculated that by 1994, the sum total of information available to humanity was going to be doubling every 18 months (and he could not have foreseen the rise of the internet so his figures were necessarily conservative). By the year 2021 he thought it would be doubling every week and later on that year it would be doubling every day.

This is the world our children are going to have to be successful in!

So the key questions our schools have to be able to answer is:

> **"What are the skills, knowledge, experience, abilities, attitudes and aptitudes our children are going to need to succeed in this world?"**

And,

> **"How can we teach them?"**

One good example of this need comes from the engineering industry. Back in the '80s I tutored in a technical university (polytechnic) in New Zealand and the engineering department there came up with some interesting figures. They had calculated that in 1964 a student enrolled in a Trade Certificate in Automotive Engineering had to become familiar with about 5000 pages of information. At that time, that student would have been expected to know most of that information, to remember it when they needed it. That information became that student's ticket, their entry into a job. By 1986 a student enrolled to complete exactly the same qualification, a Trade Certificate in Automotive Engineering, had to become familiar with 550,000 pages of information.

"One sign of insanity is doing the same thing over and over again, and expecting different results."

Albert Einstein

Now this person could no longer be expected to remember all that information, what they needed to know primarily was where to look for that information, how to sift and sort it, analyse and compare, skim and summarise.

This example represents an important shift in the focus of that student's education, from a strict focus on what to know to a focus on how to find it.

A change whereby content knowledge is no longer enough and the successful student needs high-level information processing skills as well. A shift from a total focus on content to a focus on content plus process.

This represents the challenge of today's education system. A challenge, as I see it, to raise the importance of how to learn in association with what to learn.

I am not suggesting that the content of subjects that schools teach is not important, but rather that the processes used to learn that content should be equally as important.

When students focus on the processes they are using to learn they can start to notice that small changes in process can yield big improvements in results. In my experience the biggest problem in learning failure is a lack of effective learning processes.

What our children need to learn to do is to look at the processes they use for learning and for study, decide whether those processes work for them or not, and if they don't work – change them.

Change the process - change the result.

If you think of successful learning as the outcome of the employment of effective learning processes then any learning failure can be seen as a failure of process rather than a failure of intelligence. A failure of the methods, strategies and techniques the individual is using rather than a failure of the individual themselves.

What our children all need to learn are the processes of learning, the skills, techniques and strategies of effective learning. Our children need to be taught exactly how to learn well so that they can become brilliant learners who are then able to learn from any experience or any person, from any media in any format, in any place, at any time, in any style or manner.

These are the skills that are most necessary for all our futures — *learning skills*.

Getting back to the metaphor of the centaur, the drawing back of the bow represents the readiness of the student to face the world they hurtle head on into once they leave school. The further back that string is drawn the more momentum the child has for the future. If the nature of that future world is unknowable for us, but our children have been taught how to be brilliant learners, how to use the full capacity of their own brains and minds, then it does not matter that the world is changing faster than any of us can keep up with. If your child is a brilliant learner then they will be able to cope with any new

"Things do not change; we change."

Henry David Thoreau

circumstance, they will be able to learn from any situation they find themselves in, adapt, move ahead, make changes, make progress and create success for themselves.

I think the most important thing I have ever been able to study is how people learn. I have been lucky enough to be able to research, read, study, formulate ideas, try those ideas out and measure their impact. Over the last 22 years I have studied many aspects of learning, formulated strategies to teach to teenagers and have then been able to try them out. I have kept the strategies and techniques that work well, and the rest I have discarded. Now I have an understanding of learning skills that I think can benefit any student, and we as parents have a role to play, as do teachers.

Learning Skills are the skills that your child is employing every day at school, all at different levels depending on their age and development. If your child gains competence in all of these skills by the time they finish formal schooling then you can guarantee they will be a brilliant learner able to cope with whatever the world of work and enterprise throws at them.

Some schools teach these skills directly to students and other schools rely on them picking up these skills as they learn their subjects.

I have worked in over 200 secondary schools to date in 14 different countries and I have seen maybe three or four schools who have successfully integrated their own Learning Skills programme into their curriculum. But things are changing. New Zealand, Poland, Belgium, Italy, Korea, Mexico the Slovak Republic, Spain, Canada, the USA and Turkey all have learning-skills based curricula they are presently integrating into their state school systems.

One of the most exciting developments I have been involved in recently is happening within the International Baccalaureate Organisation where the direct teaching of learning skills is being introduced into the Middle Years Programme (MYP) and called ATL (Approaches to Learning). The changes will be introduced in 2014 and if your child attends an IB school and is engaged with the MYP programme then it is possible they will get taught many of these key learning skills as they move through their programme.

This book is for all parents though, whether your child attends an IB school or not because all parents need to understand how to help their children achieve their full potential. This book has been written to give you all the ideas, strategies, techniques and skills I think are vital to helping your child or children maximize their success in all their learning endeavours.

Once teenagers have all the skills of brilliant learning, of maximising both their own potential and the potential of any situation, then the string is drawn back as far as possible and so the arrow will fly as far as possible and more importantly when it lands, no matter where it lands, no matter how complex or foreign or confusing the future is, they will cope, they will be able to take advantage of their situation and they will succeed.

"Successful people do the things that unsuccessful people don't like to do. They don't like doing them either but their purpose over-rides their dislike."

Albert E Gray

2. My Story

In my own life I think my secondary schooling did prepare me well for my subsequent life but not in any easily foreseeable manner or through any formal training or education. It is true that through a winning combination of relentless pressure, iron discipline and the cultivation of an exaggerated fear of failure, my school did manage to get me through all the necessary qualifying exams that enabled me to enter almost any university in New Zealand at the time. But I think I would have most probably been able to achieve those qualifications at any of the high schools I could have attended. It was in other areas that my particular school had a major impact on my future.

I attended a State funded boys only high school of about 500 students in the city I grew up in from Years 9-13 (Grades 8-12). At that time corporal punishment was still in vogue and masters were legally able to beat boys with a cane on any pretext. I firmly believe that this use of physical violence as punishment was what created the atmosphere of barely suppressed anger in the school that I experienced on a daily basis. In the hierarchy of students at school I was always at the bottom or next to bottom, and I spent all my years at high school being bullied, being a victim. It is still a mystery to me why in all those years I never learned how to fight back, I learned that lesson much later in life, but through that period I did learn how to endure. I think that the experience of being bullied for a long period of time had the benefit of teaching me how to be more resilient, how to cope with difficulty and how to stay fixed to my purpose.

It also helped produce within me an intense desire to escape. Since showing some aptitude in the sciences at Year 7 (Grade 6) I had been channeled along an academic pathway specialising in all three sciences, Chemistry, Physics and Biology. Not once after primary school was I exposed to learning art, music, drama or technology. By the time I finished school I had the New Zealand equivalent of A-levels or the IB Diploma in six subjects (three of them sciences), and so the logical thing for me to do was to take a Science based degree at my local university. Back in those days young people like myself were paid a generous $24/week (which was enough then to cover rent and food) to go to university through an Education Ministry awarded allowance but the government reserved the right of placement. If I wanted to do virtually any science degree I was going to be required to do at least the first year of it at the university in my home town. This meant the same situation, the same groups of young people as at school, the same trouble. I was determined to turn over a new leaf, to start a new life, to re-create myself positively. So I investigated thoroughly and discovered that there was one science degree in New Zealand that had different requirements for the first year than those that were currently offered at my local university. This was for the degree of Food Technology at Massey University in Palmerston North (200 miles away) and this is how, 5 years later, I became a fully qualified Food Technologist.

"It is the mind that maketh good or ill, that maketh wretch or happy, rich or poor."

Edmund Spenser

Now some of you may think that a food technologist is just a technical way of describing a chef or a kitchen hand, so for the sake of professional pride I need first to disabuse you of that notion and let you know that food technologists are food scientists, they are the people who in a modern world design and build everything you eat. Unless you grow it yourself in your own backyard you can guarantee a food techie or two have been involved in the process of getting it from the field to your plate. In every part of the food industry from growing through harvesting or slaughter, product development, engineering, processing, packaging, storage, marketing and distribution, food techies are involved. In my time in the industry I specialised in large-scale industrial fermentations producing, amongst other things, bakers yeast and alcohol from milk.

By the time I was 25 I was on a track to success within New Zealand's largest food processing company which was going to involve increasingly important management roles, increasing responsibilities, possible overseas postings, a company car, pension etc. But the fickle finger of fate pointed my way and prompted me to leave the industry and return to my home town for the imminent birth of my first son. I expected to get a new job quickly but after looking for a few weeks, the only thing I could find was teaching office management in the Secretarial Studies Department at the local Polytechnic. And that is how I became a teacher. I finally fell into the job that was to become my vocation, my passion. I discovered that I really enjoyed teaching, enjoyed helping other people to understand and I also discovered that teaching was a skill that I had some ability in and one that I was prepared to work hard to master. I think this was one of the most significant realisations of my life.

Teaching office management led to teaching many other things, which culminated in my taking a role educating teachers about teaching and learning. I finally discovered an intellectual challenge that I was fascinated with. How could I help young people to learn to use all of their mental faculties and capabilities more effectively, faster, better, more efficiently? That was my challenge. I read all the books, went to all the courses, searched constantly and practiced, practiced, practiced. For five years I was able to run 'accelerated learning and teaching' programmes up and down New Zealand and see many strategies I devised tested out by teachers in conventional classrooms. In the end though, due to difficulties in getting good skills transfer from teachers to students, I decided to try teaching effective learning skills directly to students themselves. I created a programme of learning skills and volunteered at a local school to run free seminars for students in the evenings over a few weeks and see if I could improve their learning performance. In the successful completion of that exercise I discovered two significant things: firstly, that students are naturally curious about their own minds and particularly interested in ways to improve their own learning ability, and secondly, that every student can improve both the effectiveness and the efficiency of their learning. No matter how successful they already were at school, after my programme they seemed to do better.

As a result of this experiment, I left my employing institution and set up my own business teaching learning skills to groups of students in high schools. And now, 20 years and 160,000 students later, I am still doing it and I think I have the best job in the world.

"Our current preoccupation with imparting knowledge must be mitigated with an energetic focus on teaching students 'how to learn', and everyone connected to education has a role to play."

Professor Guy Claxton

Teaching process, teaching the skills of effective learning, helping to draw back the string on the bow.

In so far as I can use my own example to make a point, I think that my high schooling did shape the rest of my life. The process of gaining the qualifications I achieved at school taught me how to focus, how to set goals and how to study, and the bullying I experienced taught me endurance and taught me to believe in myself. These are some of the skills all children need to get through the process of their education, especially at high school, though preferably without the trauma of a violent education.

The other thing it is possible to take from this story is the idea that linear nature of education does not suit every person. I no longer have food technology in my life, except maybe in the kitchen, and I have a degree that took 5 years of my life to achieve and another 10 years in industry to practice and discover that it wasn't what I was particularly good at or interested in. Imagine how different my life might have been if I had discovered my passion while at school or shortly after leaving there and could have then gained qualifications in the subjects I now love and love to teach 40 years later. In 2005 at 50 years old I began a Master's Degree in Education and probably for the first time in my life discovered the joy of studying something that I had a real passion for. It was interesting and enjoyable, it engaged my curiosity, I was motivated to excel and painlessly achieved 1st class honours.

My point is that in my experience, moving a child in a linear fashion from secondary school directly to university to study something that they show some aptitude in, may not be the wisest path. It is much better, I think, to help a child to get the best possible qualifications they can from school or a training organisation and then enable that child to explore both the real world and the world of ideas until they discover what they have a passion for and then have them gain good university qualifications in that area. Those children will be better able to find employment (or make employment) doing something that they love and will live more satisfying and fulfilling lives.

I am sure there are some children who are very clear about exactly what they want to do with their life from an early age but I would suggest that they are probably in the minority. Like myself, many children today do not get exposed to anything that fires their passion during their school life but they work at what they are good at and gain qualifications and often dutifully go through university and obtain a degree and end up in a job doing something that they can do well but have no abiding love for. And I guess that's 'normal' and maybe that's enough, but I think there is so much more to life than expediency.

To me the joy in life comes about from doing what fulfills you, what creates satisfaction in your heart, every day, not spending the largest part of the time in your life working at a job that you dislike so you can earn the money you need in order to enjoy your days off.

As the saying goes, *"Most people do jobs they don't enjoy, to earn money they don't need, to buy things they don't care for to impress people they don't like."*

Is that the future you want for your children?

"Learning is the key to change.
Education has to become
the single most important
investment that any person can
make in their own destiny."

Charles Handy

3. Education Is Not A Race

These days most parents tend to place a high value on education and many are willing to invest good money in the process of education. I guess that is because we want our sons and daughters to get the best possible education to enable them to qualify to go on to the best possible university to get the best possible degree to give them an advantage in the employment market to get the best job which pays the best rate and gives them a satisfying life with all their needs taken care of. However this attitude may be doing damage to our children psychologically and may be of no actual benefit to them in the professional world.

Unfortunately there is not much evidence to show that graduates from the best universities earn more money, have more interesting jobs, more job satisfaction, more influence, more power, or more happiness than other graduates and there is good evidence to the contrary – (from the USA anyway). The Wall Street Journal reports that starting salaries for 2012 graduates of Ivy League Universities were not significantly higher than those from what they termed *Engineering, Party, Liberal Arts or State universities.* Of the five groups it was the Engineering graduates from any university that were offered the highest starting salaries. Between 1998 and 2005 the percentage of CEOs of Standards & Poors top 500 companies who did not graduate from an ivy-league school rose from 84 to 90%.

Of course things may be different in other countries but in my experience the professional labour market these days is totally performance driven and good connections or a good school count for very little.

So maybe a better reason to have your son or daughter at a good school is for the exposure to a high quality teaching and learning environment which will enable them to maximise their abilities, develop all aspects of their intelligence and have the intrinsic advantages of higher level thinking and deeper understandings. Then in a performance driven working environment they can excel by virtue of their intellectual efficacy – the combination of their knowledge and skills, the talents they have developed, their attitude and their ability to learn and problem solve well.

As parents we tend to do our best to help with this process, by making sure our children are exposed to as many and as varied learning experiences as possible – the extra-curricular ballet classes, gym lessons, swimming lessons, horse riding, karate classes, piano lessons, drama classes, singing lessons, debating societies, chess clubs, not to mention extension or catch-up maths, English and other language classes. Whew! And of course we are also making sure they understand that pushing themselves to maximum effort in all that they do will help them develop the mental toughness needed to succeed in this competitive world.

"I have to say that I've always believed perfectionism is more of a disease than a quality."

Rowan Atkinson

Unfortunately much of this relentless over-achievement is simply turning into stress for our children and particularly for our daughters. One study of Year 11 students in the UK showed that over a 10 year period, while GCSE results for girls increased over boys by 10% over the same time period their rates of anxiety and depression also increased markedly. Particularly for girls from high income homes- from 24% to 38%. Interestingly enough there was no equivalent increase in mental distress amongst boys (or amongst girls from low income households) but for privileged girls the rates of hospitalisation for distress tripled – from 6% to 18%. A subsequent multi-country study of stress showed that 15-year-old girls from high income households in England are the most exam stressed students in the world (for ages 11 and 13 English girls were in second place, after the USA).

These results seem to correlate with studies of gender differences in the development of resilience. Boys have been found to exhibit significantly higher levels of discouragement and feelings of hopelessness in junior high than they do as senior students – their resilience seems to increase as they get older. Girls on the other hand seem to be more resilient than boys when they are younger but show a decrease in resilience from junior to senior high school years. Significant decreases have been found in self-regard and self-confidence of girls throughout their school development, and levels of perfectionism, hopelessness and discouragement are found to rise in girls the longer they spend in high school.

Oliver James in "Affluenza" reported an "outbreak of perfectionism in high income daughters" which I have some experience of myself . As one London inner-city private schoolgirl related to me:

"Girls have to have it all: be really, really clever, have a great social life and lots of friends, and be really pretty and thin. What leads to terribly high stress is trying to achieve all of them at once."

The perfectionist feels that her best is never good enough, she sets impossibly high standards, has an intense fear of failure and is plagued by self doubt. Perfectionism, academic success and eating disorders very often go together – in a sample of women from one Oxford University college, over one-third had suffered an eating disorder at some point in their life and 10% had one currently.

But it is not just girls who are suffering from pressure and stress – Dr Sumiya Luther from Columbia University reports

"America's newly identified 'at-risk' group is pre-teens and teens from affluent, well educated families. In spite of their economic and social advantages, they experience amongst the highest rates of depression, substance abuse, anxiety disorders, somatic complaints and unhappiness of any group of kids in this country"

"Whoever undertakes to set himself up as a judge in the field of truth and knowledge is shipwrecked by the laughter of the gods."

Albert Einstein

The significance of these studies is that on the one hand we, as parents, want our children to perform to the best of their abilities and learn to apply as much effort as possible to all their endeavours and we probably apply pressure to them to 'help' them to achieve this but on the other hand we also want them to become well balanced, resilient, confident individuals who can handle pressures and stresses with equanimity.

One way we can do this I think, is by helping our children to improve their academic confidence by moving from performance goals to process goals. Learning, to me, is the exercise of a set of skills. The more we focus on perfecting our learning skills the more effective our learning will become. From the earliest age every child needs to learn to notice how they learn as much as what they learn. To have a dual focus on content and process and practice improving the process. At school children can be encouraged to reflect on their own competence in key learning skill areas and work on improving each one up to an expert level. By the time a child leaves school we really want them to have a full set of learning skills up to the proficiency level of self-regulation, that is to have the skills necessary to be able to learn in any situation, from any person or any media, at any time, in a completely independent manner. And the funny thing is, of course, the more effective the learning processes are the better the outcomes are anyway. Win:win

In order to develop these skills our children need to practice these skills – both at school and at home. I do come across parents sometimes on my courses though who are relentlessly pushing their children from pre-school to primary school to high school to university in the belief that the faster they complete their formal education, the better off they will be. This is simply not true. Education is not a race, it's not first to finish who wins!

In January 2011, Amy Chua, a Professor of Law at Yale University, published *The Battle Hymn of the Tiger Mother,* where she espoused a philosophy of unrelenting pressure, drive, motivation, organization and planning from parents as the best way to help children achieve lofty goals. According to Prof. Chua this rigorous 'Chinese' parenting model effectively moulds children into tenacious achievers through a focus on academic results whereas more 'Western' parenting, through a focus on process and praise is much more likely to produce "unmotivated, low achieving, complacent children"

The problem with this argument is simply that the more you do for your children the less they learn to do for themselves. With the Tiger Mother philosophy it is the parent who learns and practices the key learning skills, not the child. Many children these days grow up learning how to achieve by working to an imposed regime of study rather than one of their own development and in spite of gaining academic success never really learn how to learn for themselves. Through over-supporting our children to achieve goals we may well be making them more helpless and when they need to be able to learn for themselves and by themselves, in higher education or out in the workforce, maybe they won't have the skills to enable them to do so.

Only through a process and skills focus can we help our children to become self-regulated learners.

"We are what we repeatedly do."

Aristotle

4. Three Pillars of Success - Capability, Effort and Resilience

So what are the key attributes and skills of successful self-regulated learners?

To be:

- organised, good planners
- able to focus and concentrate
- hard working – putting in the effort required at all times
- self-motivating – being able to generate their own drive no matter what the external circumstances
- creative, forward thinking
- independent – able to research, study and learn independently from any institution or teacher
- responsible – considering consequences, identifying risk
- persevering – never giving up
- self-evaluating – objectively assessing the quality of their own work
- self-correcting – able to make changes to their own processes where necessary

If you think that these are worthy attributes for a teenager finishing school, what do you think your role is in helping to create this wonderful individual?

What do you do that helps create this person? Do you ever do anything that doesn't help?

For example do you ever....

- get them out of bed
- make their breakfast – and see that they eat it
- check their school bag – make sure they haven't forgotten anything
- take them to school
- clean up after them at home
- pick them up from school
- plan out their schedule for them
- take them to after-school activities
- provide extra tutors for them
- provide motivation and rewards
- make appointments for them and see that they keep them

"It is not what you do for your children, but what you have taught them to do for themselves, that will make them successful human beings."

Ann Landers

- fight their battles for them with authority figures
- help them with their homework
- find resources for them
- make sure they go to bed on time
- organise sports, social and academic events for their weekends and holidays

Do any of these actions help them to take responsibility for their own lives and become effective decision makers and problem solvers?

It's the real parents' dilemma isn't it?

Caught between the desire to:

- take care of them, nurture them, provide for them, make their life easy, protect them from danger, provide opportunities for them, make decisions for them,

And the need to help them learn how to:

- seize opportunities, work hard, challenge themselves, overcome difficulties, take responsibility, think for themselves, become independent and make their own decisions!

All with the aim of helping them to become successful in a modern world.

So what makes for success?

Is there a magic formula?

To have success I think you have to have developed some ability – whether knowledge or skill based – to which you must add sheer hard work.

Success = Ability + Effort

Ability and Effort

There may be more to the formula but considering it so far the important question then is- *which do you think is more important in creating success, Ability or Effort?*

Because believe it or not it does make a difference. Carol Dweck, Professor of Psychology at Stanford, shows how in her 2008 book *Mindset – The New Psychology of Success.*

Covering 30 years of her research she shows how given any specific task people will naturally orient themselves into two groups. Those who think their success depends mostly on their ability and those who think their success depends mostly on their applied effort. Dweck then shows that this orientation seems to have a powerful effect on their subsequent behaviour – even at a very young age.

"It's not what you do once in a while, it's what you do day in and day out that makes a difference."

Jenny Craig

One study focussed on four year old children. First their effort/ability bias was measured, then they were given jigsaw puzzles to solve, all at the same level of difficulty.

After they had finished them, they were given the opportunity to play with more puzzles at the same level of difficulty or move on to harder puzzles.

What happened was:

- Those who thought that their effort was more important than their ability in achieving success in the jigsaw puzzles were keen to try the new, harder puzzles.
- Those who thought ability was more important than effort preferred to stay at the level that they had found success, rather than challenge themselves.

The effort-oriented children thought that solving harder puzzles would simply require more effort, something completely in their control, whereas the ability oriented children were considering the possibility that they might be at the limit of their ability already, something they considered to be outside their control. They were less likely to take a risk because of the possibility of over-reaching their ability and suffering failure.

In a failure situation the ability-oriented child is likely to think, "I can't do it", "I just don't have the ability", "I tried but obviously I can't"; whereas the effort-oriented child is likely to think "There must be a way to do it," "Next time I will watch someone else first", "Next time I will try harder"

In another study, at Columbia University, adults were given 'difficult but solvable' puzzles to solve and brain-scanned when they were given feedback on their results. The feedback was in two parts, firstly how many of the puzzles they had solved correctly, and secondly how to correct the ones they got wrong

The results were:

- Those adults who believed effort was more important than ability were very focused when they were finding out how many they got right and how many wrong and were even more focused when they were finding out what they could do to improve their results.
- Those adults who believed ability to be more important than effort were very focused when finding out how many they had got right and how many wrong but lost concentration when they were being told how to solve the puzzles they got wrong,

If we believe that ability is most important in achieving success, we seem to focus on proving that ability, whereas if we think that effort is most important, we are more likely to focus more on improving that ability.

"Genius is one percent inspiration and ninety nine percent perspiration."

Thomas Edison

In another study college students were all made to do badly in a test and then given the opportunity to look at other students' papers.

- Those who believed effort was more important than ability wanted to look at the papers of students who did better than them to see how they could improve
- Those who believed ability was more important than effort wanted to look at the papers of students who had done worse than them, to help them feel better.

It appears from the research that a belief in the primacy of effort over ability produces more persistence, a willingness to embrace challenge and a commitment to improving abilities rather than proving they still have them.

Is such a belief also fixed or can it change and develop?

Where does the belief come from?

Even more crucially: what do you think about effort vs. ability? Do you believe that ability can be improved, developed and grown, or do you think ability is fixed – in the genes? Because what you believe has a big influence on whether your children grow up believing they can grow and develop all aspects of themselves …….or not.

One last study- a group of junior high school students were given 10 puzzles to solve then divided into two groups:

- Group 1 were told that they had got an average of 8/10 right and were given praise for their ability – "you must be really smart, talented, clever, intelligent at this sort of thing"
- Group 2 were told they had got 8/10 right and were given praise for their effort – "you must be really determined, persistent, hard working, persevering with this sort of thing"

The different feedback they were given was the only difference between the two groups.

Then they were all then given the chance to work on more difficult puzzles:

Gp 1 balked – preferred to stay at the same level of difficulty
Gp 2 were keen to try harder puzzles – as with the four year olds

After trying the harder puzzles:

Gp 1's success rate dropped markedly
Gp 2's success rate dropped only slightly

The groups were then given puzzles at the original level of difficulty:

Gp 1 did worse than they had done the first time
Gp 2 did much better than they had done the first time

Praise	
... for effort "you are so hard working, persistent, determined"	**... for ability** "you are so smart, talented, intelligent"
▫ links your approval to an attribute of the child over which they have some control, one that they can grow, develop and improve ▫ assessment becomes a measure of progress, an opportunity to learn	▫ links your approval to an attribute of the child over which they have no control, one that they can't grow, develop and improve ▫ assessment becomes a critical judgement, an opportunity to fail

"Mindset" – Prof. Carol S Dweck	
Growth	**Fixed**
Intelligence, personality, talents and gifts are open to development	Intelligence, personality, talents and gifts are fixed in the genes
Effort makes the difference	The more effort you have to put in the less your ability
Failure is an opportunity to learn	Failure is catastrophic
Focus is on improving	Focus is on proving

Finally, having been asked to write a paragraph on how they thought the experiment had gone and include their scores, 40% of the Gp 1 students lied about their scores, boosting them consistently upwards.

So no matter what their natural inclination was, the feedback they received seemed to take precedence in their mind, orienting them in subsequent performance either towards effort or ability. It was the feedback which made the biggest difference.

The key question for parents is then, what do you tend to reinforce with your praise and other feedback at home- ability or effort?

Studies in the US show that 80% of parents believe it is important to praise a child's ability or talent in order to foster their confidence and their achievements. Unfortunately, praise for ability locks the child into continually having to prove that the ability is still there and still good enough. Every assessment then becomes a critical judgement of the ability and an opportunity to be judged as not good enough. Whereas praise for effort focuses the child's mind on the possibility of improving their ability and reaching a new level. Every assessment then becomes a measure of progress and an opportunity to correct and learn from any mistakes.

Carol Dweck calls these two perspectives Mindsets. The Growth Mindset and the Fixed Mindset.

If we want to reinforce the Growth Mindset in our children we can do so through being careful about the feedback we give them in different situations.

If our children do well we can focus them back on the work they did to get there, the determination and perseverance they demonstrated and the way they have changed and grown in achieving their goal.

If our children do poorly we can ask them to map out the techniques and strategies they used to get that result and to think about the amount of effort they put in. Ask them to consider what they would do differently if they had another chance, and then make sure they get to have another go.

And if children get 100% or achieve a top mark without effort …….. we can apologise to them on behalf of the school, for wasting their time and promise to contact the school and ensure that their learning is more challenging and worthy of their effort in the future.

So what is rewarded most in your home – ability or effort?

Can you organise approval in your home that advantages effort over outcome?

For example, if you like to reward your children for doing well in their exams when do you reward them? The moment they have finished their last exam? Or do you wait until the results come out in the mail and give them a suitable reward depending on the grades they achieved? The first is rewarding effort, the second is rewarding outcome. Rewarding effort seems to produce much better results long-term.

"Man is not the creature of circumstances. Circumstances are the creatures of men."

Benjamin Disraeli

Similarly we see the same behaviour showing up in students' reactions to failure. When the effort-oriented student gets 40% on a test she will look back at the process she used to get that result and will find the faults in her process – not enough effort, wrong strategy used, wrong information gathered – she will then put in place means to change the process to a more effective process for the next occurrence. The ability-oriented student on the other hand when faced with a 40% result will say something to himself like "I guess I am just not smart enough for this", he will not change his process at all and he will be likely to give up the task or the subject altogether, eventually.

So what happens in your home when your son or daughter comes home with a failed assessment? What is your reaction? Is it criticising their performance, scolding them, distracting them, comforting them or is it helping them to work out "how did I get that result – what process did I use?" And then "what could I do differently next time?" - reinforcing the successful strategies and changing the unsuccessful strategies?

As parents what we need to do is to invite our children to identify more with the effort they put in rather than with their natural ability as being the main determinant of their success.

We can do that by noticing moments when that identity is expressed:

> "I couldn't help noticing what a hard working, persistent, determined person you are"

Rather than

> "You are such a smart, talented, intelligent person"

Connect your approval to something over which they know have some control, their effort, rather than something over which they probably think they have little or no control – their abilities.

The trick is to catch them working hard at something. It doesn't matter at what as long as you can see they are putting effort into it. Help them to notice the connection between effort and outcome.

> "Did you notice how much you achieve in football (ballet, model making, learning guitar, piano etc) when you practice and train really hard"

This is where interests and passions have a part to play. The great thing about having a passion for something is that you experience what it is like to apply 100% effort. This is where you are totally focused on what you are doing because you love it so much. You see people get this way about sports, dance, music, painting, sculpture, design and many other practical things but also about areas of intellectual interest, investigating, problem solving, researching, reading, writing etc.

"Concerning all acts of initiative and creation, there is one elementary truth - that the moment one definitely commits oneself, then Providence moves, too."

Goethe

In that state known as a peak experience or flow-state we get to experience what we are really capable of. So many people never find out what is possible for them because they never experience what it is like to put 100% effort into something

Engagement with a passionate interest also generates persistence and perseverance. If your child is intrinsically motivated to learn how to play a particular sport or a musical instrument, or to learn to dance, draw, sing etc. then one thing you can do is help them to notice the internal resources they are drawing on that they use to stay focused, learn from their mistakes, push themselves to greater effort and to cope with any difficulties that arise. If they can map out the mental strategies they use when engaging with their passion, then the next step is for them to try to use the same strategies when they are doing something they enjoy less – like study. The strategies should stay the same as the situation differs. It is in learning how to get themselves do things they don't want to do that children learn to achieve.

In my country, New Zealand, schools often use participation in sport to provide this experience. Children learn through their sport how to generate intrinsic motivation and get themselves to put in 100% effort. Once they have this experience they often find it easier to push themselves to greater effort in other areas like schoolwork. In fact we often find that the students who are very dedicated to their sport are often the top academic achievers as well. Unfortunately in many other countries children are allowed to opt out of sport or sport has been taken out of the curriculum due to concerns about injuries.

Malcolm Gladwell in his book *Outliers* talks about what appears to be the universal necessity to put in the hours to achieve virtuoso level in any field. Gladwell (taking an idea from K. Anders Ericsson) quantifies this effort as 10,000 hours. This is the time it takes to become a world class tennis player, chess player, violinist, biologist, physicist, author, poet, painter, teacher, physician .... To give you some idea of how long that is think of two hours a day, five days a week for 20 years! Or three hours a day, seven days a week for 10 years.

One problem with today's instant gratification *Idol* culture is that it gives young people the impression that fame and fortune can be achieved overnight with minimum effort. One thing I often ask young people to do is to investigate the biography of someone famous that they admire. What they usually discover, often to their amazement, is the evidence of the long years of unrelenting toil that the person put in before they became famous.

Effort is king. Practise, practise, practise.

The other important aspect of Carol Dweck's work involved beliefs about intelligence. She found that students, who believe their intelligence is a fixed attribute with a definite limit, tend to avoid challenges to their intelligence. They set goals only in areas in which they already feel competent and will do whatever they can in order to avoid failure, gain approval or avoid disapproval.

In situations where they have to face serious challenges or where they suffer failure they tend to blame their own inadequacies, they feel that they can never improve in that area and they may as well give up – often abandoning both the task and the subject itself.

"Our life is what our thoughts make it."

Marcus Aurelius

Students who believe intelligence is malleable, on the other hand, enjoy challenging their own intelligence in order to develop new skills because they believe that the more they learn, the smarter they get. These students expect to suffer some failure on the way to success but they know that if they focus on improving their process and applying more effort they can succeed. They get more pleasure from achieving a task they've worked hard at than from gaining an easy success.

In one fascinating series of experiments, two groups of students reading supposedly random text for a reading comprehension exercise were in fact each processing very specific but subtly different articles. One group's article suggested that intelligence was a fixed attribute while the other group's article suggested that it was malleable. After the reading comprehension exercise was finished the students were then exposed to a series of different learning challenges, seemingly unrelated to the reading exercise. It was found in all studies that those who had read the text suggesting that intelligence was malleable, were subsequently interested in taking on more challenging learning tasks and actively took advantage of any opportunities to improve their skills that came their way. On the other hand those who had read the text suggesting that intelligence was a fixed attribute, were not as keen to increase the difficulties of the tasks, they became much more concerned about looking smart and they sacrificed learning opportunities when there was a threat of exposing their deficiencies.

Just the suggestion of an orientation towards intelligence being fixed or flexible was enough to produce quite different behaviours in response to challenge.

Suggestion influences belief and if you believe that your intelligence is something that you can develop and grow, you are much more likely to put effort into expanding, developing and growing that intelligence than if you believe it is fixed and can never develop or improve.

Learning is a process of change, of gathering information, assessing situations, understanding ideas and making adjustments to your skill or knowledge base as a result. Your whole learning process is predicated on the belief that change is possible for you. You have to first believe that you can change in order to take steps to do so.

"Competence is about dealing with familiar problems in familiar situations while capability is about the capacity to deal with unfamiliar problems in unfamiliar situations. The development of capability is best achieved by improving the processes by which people learn."

Professor John Stevenson

Getting back to my success formula.

Success = Ability + Effort?

One problem I have with the word Ability is that it suggests something given, something obvious and something finite and as we know many abilities are more latent than that and only appear when situations call for them. For this reason I like to change the word Ability to Capability to suggest more about potential than fixed attributes. So then my formula becomes:

Success = Capability + Effort

Much better but still lacking something I think. A child could have great capability and add to it considerable effort but if the first time they had a setback of some kind, got knocked down, if they stayed knocked down, gave up, then they would still be very unlikely to become successful.

I think the missing factor is Resilience, the ability to get back up again when you have a setback or a failure, and have another go.

Success = Capability + Effort + Resilience!

"We will either find a way, or make one."

Hannibal

5. Two Axes of Resilience – Learned Helplessness and Locus of Control

What is resilience?

The experts have many different things to say about the characteristics of resilient children:

"the internal assets of resilient children are those that seem to enable them to handle adversity in a positive way and to create success for themselves through their own actions" (Howard, Johnson & Oswald, 2003)

"...self efficacy, learner resourcefulness, optimism, constructive thinking" (Lazarus, 2001)

"...high self concept, internal Locus of Control, good self efficacy, self understanding, strong belief in themselves" (Maker & Neilsen 1996)

"...perseverance, persistence and optimism" (Floyd, 1996)

"...task mastery, self efficacy, internality, achievement motivation, persistence, hopefulness and optimism" (Benard, 2005)

Are these some of the characteristics that you would like to see in your children?

To me resilience is the characteristic of standing up again each time you fall over, persisting in the face of obstacles and challenges, learning from mistakes and not being put off by setbacks or failures. Research in many fields shows that resilience is the key characteristic that predisposes students to complete school, to complete university, to pursue top careers or become successful entrepreneurs and to maintain both stable long term relationships and stable mental health.

Now what I have termed a characteristic some of us would probably consider to be an attitude or a factor of personality, an individual difference produced somewhat by genetic predisposition and somewhat by environmental reinforcement. But I think that the most interesting thing I have learned in working with many thousands of students is that resilience is definitely an attitude, a state of mind, but it is a learned attitude.

And if it can be learned, then it can be taught.

"The greatest glory in living lies not in never falling, but in rising every time we fall."

Nelson Mandela

Development

The first to academically study resilience was Norman Garmezy from Minnesota University. In 1974 he studied the children of diagnosed psychopathic schizophrenics, and he found some who were actively resisting the adverse effects of their parents' mental unwellness. These children, in spite of the challenges they faced on a daily basis, had managed to develop adaptive and healthy patterns of behaviour.

And that's all resilience is really, isn't it? The trait of managing adversity well.

In the seventies resilience was largely seen as a fixed attribute genetically predetermined and evinced only in some children. By the eighties research was favouring more of a fluid concept of resilience as positive adaptation despite adversity. Not something permanent, but rather a developmental progression with new vulnerabilities and strengths emerging with changing life circumstances.

The development of resilience was the subject of my Master's thesis[1], for which I read many hundreds of papers in this field. What struck me most about those papers were three common factors:

1. the same skill/attribute set in every resilient child,
2. the importance of parents, and
3. the dearth of information on how to develop resilience.

Lots of information on what it is, very little on how to make it happen.

All resilient children have internal assets such as problem solving skills, autonomy, a purposeful, constructive and optimistic outlook on the future, effective communication and relationship skills, an internal locus of control, self efficacy, optimism, a sense of personal responsibility and purpose and a willingness to work hard. But where do they get this from?

The answer is that they get it largely from us – their parents.

It is from us that they harvest reactions to situations. It is from us that they learn how to deal with difficulties, setbacks and obstacles in their lives. It is from us that they learn habits of resilience or of helplessness.

---

1 The full thesis can be found at http://www.taolearn.com/articles/article28.pdf

"You can do anything you decide to do. You can act to change and control your life; and the procedure, the process, is its own reward."

Amelia Earhart

Control

Resilience appears to have two main theoretical components or axes, if we are thinking about this graphically. The first is Locus of Control (LOC). This model was first developed by Julian Rotter in 1966 and in the 50 years of research since then has proved to be very robust.

Your LOC is a measure of your belief in your ability to take action to affect your own life.

The scale ranges from the very Internal, who maintain complete control over every aspect of their own lives (and often other people's lives as well), to the very External – who believe that the control in their lives is completely out of their own hands.

 Where do you fit on this scale, do you think?

Try these questions:

1) You are in a taxi in a big city when it stops in traffic and waits, about 1/2 mile from your destination, 10 minutes pass with no movement.

    Do you:
    a)   just wait patiently
    b)   pay off the taxi, get out and walk
    c)   get out, walk to the front of the traffic jam, find out what the problem is, fix it, get back in your taxi and move on?

2) You are on the footpath and someone is struggling to parallel park their car.

    Do you:
    a)   keep on walking
    b)   guide them in using hand signals
    c)   tell them to get out so you can park it for them?

3) You are in a project team at work. What is your normal role?
    a)   leave it up to everyone else to do all the work
    b)   focus on doing your own part only
    c)   keep constantly checking on everyone else's work to make sure it all gets done properly?

4) Your family is going overseas for the next school holidays. What is your normal role?
    a)   let someone else organise everything
    b)   organise the flights and accommodation and make sure everyone in the family knows what they need to do to get ready

"He who knows much about others may be learned, but he who understands himself is more intelligent. He who controls others may be powerful, but he who has mastered himself is mightier still."

Lao-Tsu

c)   pack everyone's bags for them, organise every minute of the holiday, keep hold of everyone's passport and tickets and herd them all along like sheep?

Mostly a's – very external LOC

Mostly b's – moderately internal

Mostly c's – very internal LOC

Most people are somewhere in between the extremes of course but the research clearly shows that (up to a point) having a more Internal LOC is very beneficial if you want to have success in studying and learning.

To quote the experts:

> *"Internality seems to predispose students towards academic success. Students with higher academic grades scored higher on internality and lower on externality" (Park & Kim, 1998)*

> *"The three most prominent factors associated with degree attainment were academic aspiration, organisational skill and [internal] locus of control" (Suh & Suh, 2006)*

> *"Those students who entered university with lower scores on the locus of control scale [more internal] obtained significantly higher GPAs than those who scored higher [more external] on the same scale" (Gifford, Briceno-Perriot & Mizano, 2006)*

> *"The implications [of an external locus of control] are uniformly negative, as externality is correlated with poor school achievement, helplessness, ineffective stress management, decreased self-control and depression" (Twenge, Zhang & Im, 2004)*

The student with an internal LOC is going to be the one who takes charge of their own learning, who makes sure they have the best organisation, the best learning techniques and all the right information they need to succeed. The more external student will be more likely to consider that academic success or failure is out of their hands and leave it all up to fate or luck to decide.

The control that a person actually has or perceives they have is cited often in the literature as the most significant determinant of helpless or resilient behaviour. Actual control comes out of noticing causal relationships and taking action where possible to influence those relationships. Perceptions of control are more about expectations.

"There is nothing either good or bad, but thinking makes it so."

William Shakespeare

Interestingly enough there is some research to suggest that some students (in the USA at least) believe that their lives are more and more controlled by outside forces. In the forty-two years from 1960 to 2002 the externality of the average US college student increased by 80%. Given the events of September 2001, it is I guess, not surprising that there have been generalisations in attributions made across the (USA) community that have resulted in the increased belief that events are out of the control of the average person. Unfortunately the implications are uniformly negative, as externality correlates with decreased self-control, poor school achievement, helplessness, ineffective stress management, and depression.

Expectation & Attribution

Our expectations of success or failure are related directly to our attributions. These are the messages we give ourselves about the causes of things that affect our lives. In your own life what do you attribute as the cause of that flat tyre you got, that job you missed out on, that poor appraisal you received? Any negative event you experienced, what did you tell yourself was the cause?

Attributions have three common dimensions:

1. location – are you attributing the cause as something inside or outside of you?
2. stability- is the cause fixed and stable or changeable?
3. controllability- can you influence the cause?

Students who attribute success and failure to internal, unstable but controllable causes develop an expectation of success and are much more likely to take action to produce positive outcomes.

Students who attribute success and failure to causes outside themselves which are fixed and over which they have no control are much more likely to feel helpless and to develop expectations of failure.

If someone believes they have some control over their task outcomes they are more likely to persevere, put in effort, learn from mistakes and take action to produce the result they want.

But what are the factors that produce an internal locus of control with respect to learning at school?

For a student to increase their internality, the necessary conditions are for them to:

1. have some experience of taking control of their own learning
2. gain some success from doing so and
3. notice the connection.

"If you are distressed by anything
external, the pain is not due
to the thing itself but to your
own estimate of it; and this you
have the power to revoke at any
moment."

Marcus Aurelius

This then allows the student to build more personal attributions of successful control, greater expectations of academic success and leads to more successful, and more effective learning.

So when you think about the learning that your child is doing at school, what are the factors that they can exert some control over?

- what to learn?
- when to learn?
- how to be taught?
- what media they are taught through?
- who they can learn with?
- what is in the tests and assignments?
- the criteria for assessment?
- the standards to which they are assessed?
- the timing of assessments?
- the format of assessments?
- the marking of their tests and assignments?
- the grades they are awarded?

When you think about their schooling from the point of view of control there is very little in their entire learning experience that is totally in their control.

Unfortunately for the more externally oriented student, when they suffer any kind of setback or failure they tend to attribute that failure to one of the things they have no control over. It's always the teacher's fault, the other students' fault, the textbook's fault, the weather's fault. Anything but them. In making these attributions they are relieving themselves of any responsibility to take positive action to effect their own success but unfortunately all that means is that they don't learn from their experiences, mistakes and setbacks and they are then doomed to repeat them.

To my mind there are two principle factors that influence a student's learning over which they can exert control- effort and strategy use. By strategy use I mean the learning techniques they use when they are learning at school and at home. How they learn, the techniques they employ, the learning skills they have mastered to process the information they receive at school in order to understand and recall it. By effort I mean simply that, hard work, sweat, hours put in.

Effort and strategy use are the two key factors most influencing a student's achievement in learning which are internal, open to change and controllable. These then are the two factors to focus on if we would like our children to have more success at school.

"Nothing can resist the human will that will stake even its existence on its stated purpose."

Benjamin Disraeli

I have talked about effort in the last section. Strategy use will be covered in a later chapter. The important thing to realise at this point is that by exerting influence over the things that they can control, students can begin to become more internal in LOC orientation.

Step 1 involves your children identifying the things that they can have greatest influence over. Step 2 involves them taking on the responsibility for influencing those factors through positive action.

Learned Helplessness

The other theoretical model that contributes to our present day understanding of resilience is that of Learned Helplessness, developed by Martin P. Seligman – Professor of Psychology at Pennsylvania State University.

Learned helplessness is that feeling that you get when it's Friday night, late, you are finally going home from work having put in a big week and you're bone tired and it's raining, cold and wet and the train breaks down or the plane is delayed for hours, or the weather turns worse or there is a strike and you're stuck – in a train station or an airport. You're trying to get home and you're stuck- it's desperately miserable and there's nothing you can do.

The conditions that are most likely to bring about feelings of helplessness are when someone:

- is feeling distressed,
- cannot understand why the distress is happening to them,
- cannot influence or affect the nature or the level of the distress,
- and cannot escape – they have to endure

For some people their working life is like this and for some students their school life is like this.

Learned helplessness was first conceived of in 1975 and the 33 years of research since then have clearly shown that helplessness is not a useful attribute for the successful student.

> *"...the characteristics are inattention, difficulty in thinking, depression, giving up in the face of failure, pessimistic attitude, self criticism, self blame, inability to persist or persevere" (Seligman, 1975)*

> *"...those who perceive bad events to be pervasive, permanent and caused by themselves become helpless and depressed and may give up trying" (Dunn & De Saintongue, 1998)*

"A person is not hurt so much by what happens as by their opinion of what happens."

Michael de Montaigne

"Learned helplessness is characterised by an unwillingness on the part of the student to engage in tasks because he or she believes that effort is futile and failure is imminent" (Seifert, 2004)

"When people experience learned helplessness, they have a tendency to give up easily or fail more often at somewhat easier tasks" (Firmin et al, 2004)

The characteristics of learned helplessness seem to be exactly opposite to those of resilience, don't they?

Helplessness is essentially the inability to take action to affect your own life. This inability may be because an external agent has taken away all your options for action, as occurs in rigid military establishments, some schools, prisons and prison camps, or it may simply be because you believe you have no options. Helplessness is an important attribute to cultivate if your aim is to generate subservience. Resilience is the ability to overcome helplessness.

A deterioration in academic performance due to helplessness has been shown to be induced simply by giving students unsolvable puzzles and telling them they need to solve them to pass. Or by giving students problems they just can't solve as the first problems to face in an exam. In these cases it is not the removal of all their options for action, but simply creating the expectation of failure that produced helplessness and the deterioration of academic performance.

We all have a tendency to feel helpless occasionally but people vary in both the frequency and depth of those feelings. This tendency towards or away from helplessness can be measured, according to Seligman, by analysing a persons reactions to good and bad luck. The nature of these reactions reveals the tendency to adopt pessimistic or optimistic thinking. Pessimistic thinking has been found to correlate well with helplessness and Seligman correlates optimistic thinking with resilience.

Test yourself with the following scenarios. In each case read the situation statement first, then think about what your initial reaction would be – what would you would say to yourself in the moment of that particular circúmstance? Then compare your response with the two given below each question.

1. You park in a carpark building and go shopping. When you return you see that there is now a big crease all the way down one side of your car where someone has crashed into you.

   What do you say to yourself?
   a) "This is all my fault, I knew I shouldn't park here"
   b) "Some idiot has run into my car! Where is the carpark attendant, he should have prevented this.

"We are what we think.

All that we are arises.

With our thoughts.

With our thoughts,

We make the world."

Buddha

2. As you get closer to the car you notice that you have also got a flat tyre and you know you don't have a spare.

    What do you say to yourself now?
    a) "OK, that's enough bad luck, something good has to happen now"
    b) "Why does this always happen to me? I knew I should have replaced that spare tyre."

3. You manage finally to wrench the driver's door open and as you do something falls down from behind the dash onto the floor. You pick it up and discover it is a piece of jewellery of great personal value that you had thought was lost which because of the crash has now been found.

    What do you say to yourself now?
    a) "Even my bad luck is good"
    b) "Maybe I should find the culprit and thank him for crashing into me"

4. You settle into the car and notice a piece of paper that is stuck under the windscreen wiper. You read it and see it is from whoever crashed into your car offering to pay to fix up your car and also to lend you another car until yours is fixed.

    What do you say to yourself?
    a) "What a fluke. That won't ever happen again"
    b) "I knew it would all come out right in the end

Optimistic responses: 1b, 2a, 3a, 4b
Pessimistic responses: 1a, 2b, 3b, 4a

Optimistic responses in almost all practical situations produce more favourable outcomes than pessimistic responses, including in medical situations. After breast cancer surgery, optimistic thinkers have been found to recover faster, be less likely to develop complications and to maintain better physical health five years later than pessimistic thinkers. Optimistic thinkers are also more likely to maintain a healthy eating programme, reduce their intake of saturated fat, take up exercise and reduce body fat. They are more likely to complete an alcohol abuse rehabilitation programme and less likely to commit suicide. Optimistic thinkers seem to be both better able to accept the reality of an uncontrollable situation than pessimistic thinkers, and to be more solution-focused in their planning and acceptance of treatment. Pessimistic thinkers tend to engage in much more denial and escapism.

"It is not events that shape our lives but our response to those events."

Lance King

Habitually optimistic thinkers also have

- less depression and mental illness
- longer life
- more happiness
- and are more resilient after setbacks

than habitually pessimistic thinkers.

But habitually optimistic thinkers are also

- less accurate judges of their own abilities
- less accurate judges of their own influence over events
- more inclined to take risks and
- more inclined to blame others for their own failings

than more pessimistic thinkers

And this is where an unvaryingly optimistic outlook can sometimes prove to be detrimental. Optimistic thinkers often overestimate their own capabilities, underestimate risks and when things go bad, blame others for their own mistakes.

But in all other respects optimistic thinking produces the most resilient response in any given situation especially trying and troubling ones. To be able to generate an optimistic outlook when you are in great difficulty is a universally admired trait often found in great leaders, great sportspeople and great educators.

If we could somehow blend together the advantages of an optimistic outlook, with the need to take responsibility for your own mistakes, and the ability to take positive action, we might have an unbeatably resilient persona.

If you put these two ideas together – the Locus of Control and the Learned Helplessness - graphically, on different axes, you get four different segments which make up the **Gnostates.**

"The only person you are destined to become is the person you decide to be."

Ralph Waldo Emerson

6. The Gnostates

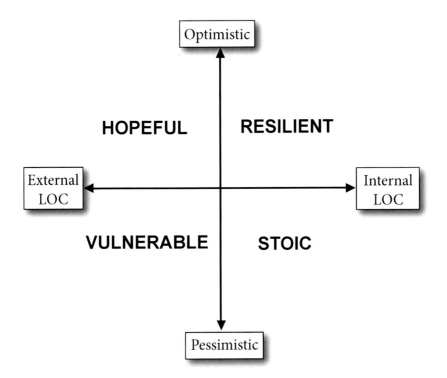

These I call the **Gnostates**- from the Greek gnosis meaning self knowing. Each quadrant is a different state of self-knowing – or self-gnowing.

Top right we have the **Resilient** – willing to take action to affect their own lives and optimistic about the outcome. They are indomitable, they get back up every time they get knocked down, they learn from their mistakes and consistently move ahead – our best entrepreneurs, explorers, adventurers fit in here.

Top left we have what I call the **Hopeful** – unwilling to take action to affect their own lives but optimistic about the outcome. They are quite convinced everything is going to be OK, fine, no problem, but are unprepared to do anything to help achieve that result.

In my experience this is a characteristic 14 year old boy syndrome- "It'll be fine mum, I'll be OK, no problem, I'll pass easily, no need to study, don't worry...."

"I know of no more encouraging
fact than the unquestionable
ability of man to elevate his life
by conscious endeavour."

Henry David Thoreau

Bottom right we have what I call the **Stoic** – prepared to take action to affect their own lives but pessimistic about the outcome. They consider that working hard is a natural part of life but they don't really expect it to turn out that well for them. They are solid, reliable conservative, risk avoiders, not adventurous and often controlling of others.

And bottom left we have the **Vulnerable** - not prepared to take action to affect their own lives and pessimistic about the outcome. They feel powerless to change their life and they expect the worst to happen. Depressed, helpless- "it's all going bad and there's nothing I can do."

The most important thing to realise at this point is that both locus of control and learned helplessness patterns of thinking are learned responses to situations which can be un-learned. **Wherever you are on the gnostates grid IT IS POSSIBLE TO MOVE, TO CHANGE, TO GROW.**

And the real challenge, if you want the resilient characteristics in your children, is to help them move towards the resilient quadrant – from wherever they are. We can do this by helping them to practise optimisitic thinking but also help them to take responsibility and control, especially in situations where they have made mistakes or experienced failure. More on this later.

If you would like to take the Gnostates test yourself I have included here the two quizzes from the adults' version of the Gnostates analysis. There are two quizzes to complete. Each one will yield one answer between 0 and 18 which will place you along one axis of the Gnostates grid. Then the intersection of the two scores will place you in one segment of the Gnostates Grid.

Gnostates Quiz One – Marking Schedule

1a – 1	1b – 0
2a – 0	2b – 1
3a – 1	3b – 0
4a – 0	4b – 1
5a – 1	5b – 0
6a – 1	6b – 0
7a – 0	7b – 1
8a – 1	8b – 0
9a – 1	9b – 0
10a – 0	10b – 1
11a – 0	11b – 1
12a – 0	12b – 1
13a – 1	13b- 0
14a – 0	14b – 1
15a – 1	15b – 0
16a – 0	16b – 1
17a – 1	17b – 0
18a – 0	18b – 1

This score gives you a place between 1 and 18 on the vertical Optimism/Pessimism axis of the Gnostates grid (see page 80)

Gnostates Quiz Two – Marking Schedule

1a – 0	1b – 1
2a – 1	2b – 0
3a – 1	3b – 0
4a – 0	4b – 1
5a – 0	5b – 1
6a – 1	6b – 0
7a – 0	7b – 1
8a – 1	8b – 0
9a – 1	9b – 0
10a – 1	10b – 0
11a – 0	11b – 1
12a – 1	12b – 0
13a – 0	13b- 1
14a – 0	14b – 1
15a – 0	15b – 1
16a – 1	16b – 0
17a – 1	17b – 0
18a – 0	18b – 1

This score gives you a place between 0 and 18 on the horizontal Locus Of Control axis of the Gnostates grid (see page 80)

Gnostates Quiz One

In the following hypothetical situations choose your more likely response from the two responses provided:

1. The project you are in charge of is a great success:
    a) My hard work and energy got us through
    b) Without the others I couldn't have done it

2. You and your partner make up after an argument:
    a) I hope the good mood lasts
    b) With us the bad moods never last

3. You get lost driving to an acquaintance's house:
    a) My directions must be wrong
    b) I must have missed a turn

4. Your spouse (boy/girlfriend) surprises you with a gift:
    a) I wonder what s/he wants?
    b) I deserve this

5. You forget an important birthday/anniversary date
    a) I have remembered all his/her other important dates
    b) I'm just no good at remembering dates

6. You get a card from a secret admirer:
    a) People like me
    b) Somebody likes me

7. You run for a place on your local community board and you win:
    a) I guess I was the right person at the right time
    b) I work very hard to achieve what I want

8. You miss an important engagement:
    a) I am under too much pressure
    b) I forgot to check my diary this morning

9. You run for a place on your local community board and you lose:
    a) I didn't work and campaign hard enough
    b) The person who won had more contacts than me

Gnostates Example 1 - Score 6 on Quiz One

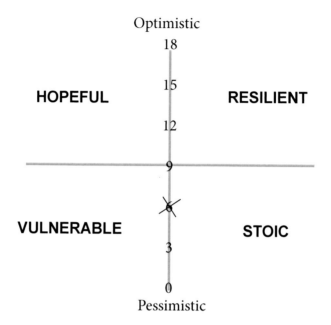

Gnostates Example 1 - and then score 12 on Quiz Two

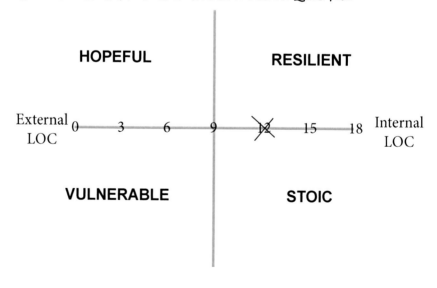

10. You host a successful dinner party:
    a) I was in great form that night
    b) I am a great host

11. You hear a crash next door and stop a crime by calling the police:
    a) It was lucky they were so clumsy
    b) I am always prepared to take action on my suspicions

12. You owe the library ten dollars for an overdue book:
    a) I always forget to take my books back
    b) I was so involved in writing the report that I forgot to return the book

13. You go to the casino and win some money:
    a) I was lucky the game was so easy
    b) What an easy way to make money

14. You fail an important exam:
    a) I wasn't as smart as the other people taking the exam
    b) I didn't prepare for it well enough

15. You prepare a special meal for a friend and he/she barely touches the food:
    a) Maybe s/he is not feeling well tonight
    b) Now the whole night is ruined

16. Your car runs out of gas late at night.
    a) I didn't check the petrol gauge when I got in
    b) The petrol gauge must be faulty

17. You lose your temper with a friend
    a) S/he made me mad
    b) S/he is always nagging me

18. Your boss gives you too little time in which to finish a project, but you get it finished anyway.
    a) I'm glad I got that out of the way
    b) I always like to finish what I start

Gnostates Example 1 - Join the points together

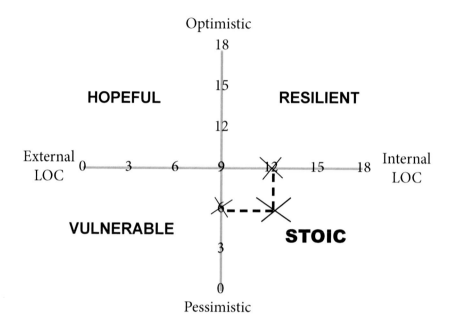

Combined result places Example 1 in the STOIC quadrant

Now do the second quiz – Gnostates 2:

Gnostates Quiz Two

In the following pairs of statements chose the one that is closest to what you think is generally true:

1. a) Most of the unhappy things in people's lives are due to bad luck
   b) People's misfortunes usually result from bad decisions they make

2. a) One of the major reasons why we have wars is because people don't take enough interest in politics
   b) There will always be wars, no matter how hard people try to prevent them

3. a) In the long run, people get the respect they deserve in this world
   b) An individual's worth often passes unrecognised no matter how hard s/he tries

4. a) Most school teachers are biased in their assessment marking towards some students and against others
   b) Most school teachers mark all assessment papers fairly

5. a) Without good luck, one cannot be an effective leader
   b) Ambitious, capable people who fail to become leaders have not taken advantage of their opportunities

6. a) In the past when I have failed to achieve a goal I have set for myself it has usually been because I have made a bad decision
   b) In the past when I have failed to achieve a goal I have set for myself it has usually been because of factors outside my control

7. a) What is going to happen will happen
   b) Trusting to fate has never turned out as well for me as making a decision to take a definite course of action

8. a) For the well prepared student, there is no such thing as an unfair exam
   b) Exam questions frequently tend to be so unrelated to course work that a lot of studying makes little or no difference

9. a) Becoming a success is mostly a matter of hard work, luck has little to do with it
   b) Success mainly depends on being in the right place at the right time

10. a) The average citizen can have an influence on government decisions
    b) This world is run by a few people in power and there is virtually nothing any one person can do about it

Your Scores - mark in your results on this graph and join the points together and find which quadrant you end up in

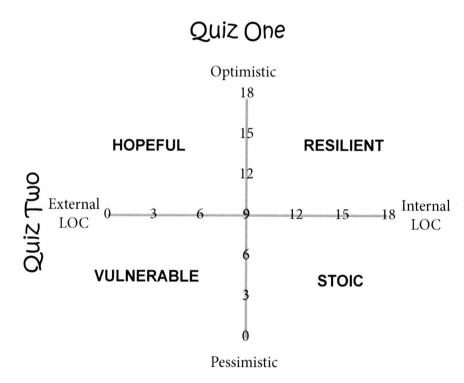

11. a)   I have found that it is best not to plan too far ahead because other things always get in the way of completing plans I make

    b)   When I make plans, I really try to stick to them and do everything I can to make them work

12. a)   When making decisions I like to analyse all aspects of the situation

    b)   When making decisions I prefer to go with my gut feeling

13. a)   When I am working in a team I prefer someone else to take charge

    b)   When I am working in a team I like to personally ensure that everything is done properly

14. a)   Sometimes I feel that I don't have any control over the direction my life is taking

    b)   What happens to me is my own doing

15. a)   When I make a mistake the most important thing is to not let it slow me down – to ignore it and keep on going

    b)   When I make a mistake the most important thing is to find out what I did wrong and change something to make sure I can't make that mistake again

16. a)   If my boss is putting pressure on me to change my mind over something I usually stick to my own views

    b)   If my boss is putting pressure on me to change my mind over something I usually go along with what s/he wants

17. a)   If I am travelling with my family I organise everything

    b)   If I am travelling with my family I let each member organise themselves

18. a)   for appointments I am sometimes late

    b)   for appointments I am always either early or exactly on time

82

be more optimistic

HOPEFUL
- positive
- easy-going
- high risk taker
- procrastinator
- takes easy option
- self-promoting

RESILIENT
- leader
- bounces back
- takes charge
- always learning
- calculated risks
- self-motivated

take more control

- accepting
- passive
- depressed
- "I can't"
- helpless
- self-limiting

- controlling
- reliable
- diligent
- pessimistic
- frustrated
- self-blaming

VULNERABLE   ## STOIC

In this book we can only do a very crude analysis of your Gnostate that places you in one quadrant or another. In the full analysis, available (free on-line at **http://www.taolearn. com/gnostates/index.htm**) within each of the four quadrants there are 4 subsets depending on exactly where your two scores intersect. This is much too complicated to be included here but if you are interested in following this further and receiving a full analysis, diagnosis and strategies for change please go to the website and complete the questionnaires there. Your children can also undertake the same analysis but with versions of the questionnaires more suited to their age group.

The question remains, for parents though- how can we help our children to move away from the Vulnerable, Stoic and Hopeful quadrants and towards the Resilient quadrant?

Simply put, what they have to do is take control of the factors they can control, take responsibility for all their own actions and maintain a positive optimistic attitude.

And what we have to do is to assist them in that endeavour.

But first, did you notice that in both the LOC and LH models it was the attribution pattern of the individual that revealed their control and helplessness or resilience patterns? And where do we learn attribution patterns from? Mostly from our parents.

Think back to your own childhood. Think of one example from then of a good luck event, eg. someone got an unexpected bonus or was the recipient of unexpected generosity from someone else; and one example of a bad luck event, eg. a pet died unexpectedly or a natural event had negative consequences for your family. Now remember how those events were dealt with in your family.

Was the good luck celebrated and dwelt upon or dismissed as a random event that would never happen again?

Was the bad luck dwelt upon and agonised over or dismissed as a random never-to-be-repeated event?

Be aware that habitual attribution patterns are very powerful and are often unconsciously learned by children. Do you have similar attribution patterns to your parents? Are these the most useful patterns? Have these patterns then been passed onto your children?

Now think about other situations from your childhood. Can you think of a situation where one or both of your parents had been actively involved in a business or personal situation which did not turn out well? Where they invested time and effort in a venture in which mistakes or bad decisions were made? And in the aftermath of that situation, what did they do? Did they actively look back at that situation, take responsibility for their own actions and learn from that situation or did they dismiss it, put it behind them and carry on regardless?

"I have been impressed with the urgency of doing. Knowing is not enough; we must apply. Being willing is not enough; we must do."

Leonardo da Vinci

The resilient state of mind can be created by taking control where possible, especially control of attribution. The attributions which create resilience are those that look for positive interpretations of all situations, except where personal responsibility for mistakes must be taken. In those situations it is not a pessimistic outlook that is required, it is a pragmatic, process focused view that is most resilient:

▫ what mistakes did I make?
▫ what can I learn from my mistakes?
▫ what would I do differently next time?
▫ when can I try out my new strategy?

Resilient Learners:

1. Take a process-focused view of their own learning. This means they focus on learning goals rather than performance goals. Resilient students are learning at school to improve their knowledge and skills rather than to get "A" passes or "Excellence" grades.

2. Want to master their subjects for their own sake rather than in order to gain someone's approval or avoid someone's disapproval

So at home it is important to reinforce the intrinsic value of every subject your children learn, emphasising the relevance to today's world and your children's future life.

Also help focus your children on the usefulness of understanding and eventually mastering the particular academic discipline they are engaged in, and downplay the grade or mark as the aim of learning. Your children need to be learning for personal benefit rather than learning in order to achieve a certain score or the approval of others – be they yourself, teachers or peers. And if grades and scores are important to you be reassured that the best grades always come out of gaining a complete understanding of any subject – gaining mastery.

Resilient learners are also

3. Challenge seeking rather than challenge avoiding

What has been found in some studies is that the less resilient students actively plot a path for themselves through school that avoids all significant challenge in order to avoid ever having to experience failure. The reason being that they feel that their performance is most significantly judged by others – approval seeking or disapproval avoiding – and so the thing which is most significant for them is avoiding looking bad. Girls universally show more resilience than boys in primary and intermediate years but much less resilience than boys in secondary years due, it seems, to the developing concern with girls to look good as they get older.

"The trouble is, if you don't risk anything, you risk even more."

Erica Jong

To get past this we need to help all our children to rely more on their own judgement of their progress and success rather than the judgement of others. To compare themselves with themselves rather than with others and to be proud of their own growth, development and ability to handle new challenges. To do this we need to make sure that our children can always generate new challenges in their lives to test themselves with. So help your children to take on new challenges, to test themselves always with something that they think is more than they can do.

For example every year when my children were choosing subjects to take at school the following year I always suggested they think about taking at least one subject that they knew nothing about – one that would be totally new for them in order to maintain the challenge of learning new things.

Lastly, in all the hundreds of papers I read on the topic of resilience, the single most common factor was the presence, in every resilient child's life, of at least one committed, concerned, totally supportive adult. One adult who did not make their approval conditional on the behaviour of the child but who unconditionally supported and approved of that child because of who they were not because of what they did.

I think this is very significant because how many children have at least one adult in their lives like this? It may be a parent, a grandmother or other relative, it may be a coach, teacher, church leader, older sibling. Whoever it is does not seem to matter but the support of their unconditional regard appears to be very important for the development of resilience.

Interestingly enough most resilience research has been conducted in seriously disadvantaged populations where extremes of vulnerability produce examples of resilience most notable by their scarcity. It is in these situations where the effects of uncontrollable, external forces and the urgency of simple survival can be so overwhelming to the majority that the resilient are easy to identify. The key themes that seem to pervade virtually all resilience studies are those of people actively taking control of their own life where they can, to reduce the randomness and helplessness of their situation and at the same time maintaining an optimistic view of the possibilities that could be available for them.

"In some ways I think I epitomise
the average New Zealander - I
have modest abilities which
I combine with a good deal of
determination, and I rather like
to win."

Sir Edmund Hillary on the
occasion of his eightieth birthday

The unintentional bias in all the resilience research however is that there are no studies (that I have found), on similar developments in middle class and privileged populations. This might suggest that resilience is a characteristic only of the impoverished or the disadvantaged but common sense would suggest that it is not socio-economics that produces resilience it is something else. Resilience development appears to involve a conceptual change, a change in thinking away from helplessness towards inner strength that sometimes occurs in situations of significant risk but may also occur in situations of minimal risk.

The development of resilience is absolutely vital for all our children. Resilience confers on one the ability to cope with all of life's difficulties, to see them as challenges to be overcome, situations to be mastered and mistakes to be learned from. The development of resilience protects children from helplessness, enables them to take control where they can and helps them avoid the predation of depression.

For today's school students the development of the attribute of resilience is vital, and if it can be built into a framework of effective learning then we have the possibility of developing the resilient learner- the one who can not only cope with every problem they face but learn from it, take advantage of it and profit from their own mistakes.

Although resilience and academic success often occur together, resilience itself is not sufficient however to produce academic success, that requires the application of resilience within a framework of skills which in the broadest sense could be called the skills of effective learning.

"Success means doing the best we can with what we have. Success is the doing, not the getting; in the trying, not the triumph. Success is a personal standard, reaching for the highest that is in us, becoming all that we can be."

Zig Ziglar

7. Three Drivers Of Effective Learning

From 20 years work with over 160,000 students I have developed my own model of what it takes to become a successful, resilient, self-regulated learner which I think includes three key components:

Efficacy + Agency + Action

Efficacy is self-belief- the belief within each student that successful learning is possible for them

Agency is skills- all the skills, strategies and techniques of effective learning

Action is all about failing well – the opportunity and willingness to have a go, make mistakes and fail well

And the good news is that these three things are all things we as parents can help our children to develop!

"Some men see things as they are, and say, 'Why?' I dream things that never were, and say, 'Why not?'"

George Bernard Shaw

8. Four Foundations of Efficacy

i.   Purpose – the answer to the question "why?"

Why are your children at school?

Why is it important that they do well at school?

What do they think?

Have you asked them?

I ask this question of students on every course that I run.

It is the most fundamental question because if you don't know why you are doing something it is so much harder to get it done.

And the first reasons students from all parts of the world come up with are always the same:

- to get good qualifications
- to get into the right university
- to get a good job – usually defined as one which earns a great deal of money
- to please their parents or make their parents proud
- to prove how smart they are

All of which you might see as perfectly valid reasons. The problem with all these reason though is that they are all external to the self. And because they are external they are not particularly powerful or successful as motivators of present performance. They are useful to use as goals to be able to plan towards but they are not particularly effective drivers of excellent performance, they do not work well to keep students focused and working hard when times get tough.

The types of motivators that by their nature are within the self are the ones which generate the internal energy students need to keep task focused and working hard until they finish. These are intrinsic or internal motivators like:

- to feel satisfied, proud of yourself
- to test yourself and see what you are capable of
- to get a measure of your progress to date
- to gain knowledge and skills that will be useful to you in your life
- to develop and increase your intelligence
- to practice concentration, determination and the exercise of effort

Which are all reasons that very rarely occur to students at school.

"They can because they think they can"

Virgil

Intrinsic motivation is the drive to achieve that comes from within and doesn't need external forces to stimulate or produce it. I'm sure you know what I mean – intrinsic (or internal) motivation is working for us at any time when we feel we really want something. And it is working most powerfully for us when we are totally driven to produce or achieve something and we don't let anything stand in our way.

When it comes to our children, of course, we want them to be intrinsically motivated to concentrate in class, to do their homework, to study for tests and exams. But parents often feel that they have to provide extra motivation for their children externally with rewards and prizes. And external motivation is never as powerful as internal motivation. In order for children to understand this, they need to have experiences where they are self-motivated. Experiences, in any field, where they push themselves to achieve what they can simply because they want to, because they enjoy it. Moments when they are driven to achieve by virtue of an internally generated purpose .

If children are not clear as to the purpose of their studies it is important for parents to help them focus on internal, intrinsic motivators for study, school work and passing exams to help them develop the perseverance and persistence necessary to succeed.

ii)   Self-confidence – a feeling of personal competence

It is my contention that self-confidence is not something that we develop through competition. It is an attitude or attribute we generate by comparing ourselves with ourselves and noticing any development or improvement in the desired direction. There is nothing inherently wrong with competition, it can be a great force to harness to push ourselves to greater performance but I don't think it tends to generate self-confidence. Real self-confidence only comes from noticing that you have got better at something, that you are more competent, more skilled than you once were. Noticing that you are improving by comparing yourself with yourself, not by comparing yourself to others. "I am getting much better at this" is always going to be more affirming than "I am better than Harry but not as good as Jane".

This means that in all the things that your children are learning at school, one of the most useful records they can have is a record of their own progress – measuring themselves against themselves.

Just think for a moment. In your house is there a doorway or a wall somewhere with little marks on it getting higher and higher, with names and dates attached to each one? This is the record you made of your child's growth over time which was an important indicator for them because children don't usually notice that they are growing. They often get the feeling that everyone else is growing and leaving them behind so we make a visual chart for them to see that it is OK, that they are growing just as much as everyone else.

Now what I think we all need in our households to help our children gain self-confidence about their intellectual growth are visual records of their progress in all the things that they are learning at school.

"Be more concerned with your character than your reputation, because your character is what you really are, while your reputation is merely what others think you are."

John Wooden

Imagine if you took all the information that comes home from school about your children's progress and turned it into visual displays. Graphs or charts or pictures showing clearly that they are getting more maths problems right this month than they were last month or more spelling words right or more language proficiency or artistic or scientific proficiency this year compared to last year. If children could easily see that they were making progress in all the important measures of achievement – progress against themselves, not against anyone else – then maybe that would help them to develop more self-confidence in their ability to learn well and cope with the rigours of school.

iii) Self esteem – a feeling of self worth

If your children's self esteem is related to their feelings of worthiness or being valued within the family, the important question for parents then is: what do you value your children for? What attributes or characteristics of your children have the highest value in your home? And do you value your children as much for who they are as for what they produce? One unfortunate thing I see in some families is parents who value their children only for the scores they produce or the behaviours they exhibit which unfortunately then ties their self-esteem completely to their performance, not to themselves as people. The problem with placing too high a value in the family on outcomes or results is the effect this has on the child's feeling of self worth if they don't produce that best performance. If the child doesn't achieve that top mark, or produce that perfect behavior are they then suddenly not of any value in the family?

There is nothing wrong with valuing achievements but we need to make sure that as well as valuing the achievements of our children we also value the person they are, as separate from their achievements.

If a child is acting badly or achieving poor results – exhibiting behaviour that we as parents don't approve of – then we must be very careful to disapprove of the behaviour not of the child. The child needs to be still valued as a wonderful person but we may wish them to change their behaviour.

Parental approval is a very powerful force in shaping children's self esteem and it is instructive for most parents to look at what they approve of and disapprove of with their children.

Remember always that your child is a human-being not a human-doing. It is not what they do that distinguishes them as an individual it is the person that they are which does so.

"If your determination is fixed,
I do not counsel you to despair.
Few things are impossible to
diligence and skill. Great works
are performed not by strength,
but perseverance."

Samuel Johnson

iv) Reaction to challenges – noticing their self-talk and any attributions they make, particularly around setbacks and failures.

In my learning skills courses for students I spend some time focusing on self motivation and handling challenges. I do this is by asking children to start noticing their own internal dialogue and internal imagery, particularly in challenging situations. I then show them how they can learn to take charge of all the messages they give themselves internally and to mentally set themselves up for success.

One way I do this is through my juggling exercise. The reason I teach children how to juggle is because I use that exercise to give them a real learning challenge that they have to face up to, purely to help them to notice the reactions they have to challenges. Because if I can get them to notice their reactions then I can also teach them how to take control of their reactions. And when faced with the challenge of learning something new, taking control of your initial reactions is step one in learning successfully.

The first reaction we get students to notice when they are faced with a challenge is simply what they say to themselves inside their heads.

A person's internal dialogue and attributions are particularly evident when they experience some failure.

A lot of students have a habitual reaction to failure or challenge which is to say – out loud or just inside their head something like

"I can't ...."

What we do is get them to notice this and to deliberately make a shift in their own internal dialogue from

"I can't ....." to "I haven't yet ...."

Because words create suggestions and as you saw from Carol Dweck's effort/ability research, suggestion changes performance.

The suggestion contained in the words "I can't" is that you never ever will — it is physically impossible; learning to juggle (or sing, or dance, or do algebra or biology, or creative writing, whatever the challenge might be) is an ability of the human body that you just don't have.

Whereas the suggestion contained in the words "I haven't yet" is that you still might- that it is still possible, given more work.

"Whether you think you can or you think you can't, you're right."

Henry Ford

But notice what is happening here. By helping a child change their internal dialogue, we are helping them to shift their attribution for failure from an ability attribution — "I can't" — meaning "I just don't have the ability to, to an effort attribution "I haven't yet done it." — in other words "if I try again, if I have another go, put in more work, I might yet learn to do it."

And the effect is immediate. As soon as they change their language they change their success. I have proved this many thousands of times during my courses. We are a language dominated species, we have a language dominated brain. Taking control of your internal dialogue is the first key step to creating success, as much for yourself as for your children.

And make sure you provide the example by eliminating all your own "I can'ts" and replacing them with "maybe I just haven't yet".

So what I suggest you do for your children is to start to listen to what they say when they have some failure or are faced with a challenge to do something that is more than they think they can do. Notice what they say, and encourage them to shift their language from a focus on their ability to a focus on their effort.

Not from "I can't" to "I can" but from "I can't to "I haven't yet".

Noticing what they say to themselves is step one, and taking control of what they say to themselves is step two in your children setting themselves up to achieve success.

"Experience is learning, all else is information."

Albert Einstein

9. The Three Skills Of Agency - Cognitive, Affective, Metacognitive

As I discussed earlier, by learning skills I mean the strategies, techniques and methods your children are using when they are doing their homework, doing assignments, learning schoolwork, and studying for tests and exams. When I was young, learning effectively was assumed to be a natural consequence of high intelligence. If someone wasn't good at studying then obviously they were just not smart enough. Modern theories of learning and intelligence however show that this is not the case at all. The plasticity and growth potential of both brain and mind are now widely accepted ideas. Effective study is now known to be the result of the application of effective strategies and techniques that come from the mastery of good learning skills.

And do most students have those learning skills?

In some studies up to 73% of university students have been found to use weak or ineffective strategies for processing information in their own study, in lectures or tutorials and also when studying for an exam.

If we just look at note-making, it is easy to see that good note making is important for academic achievement and yet when making notes from lectures or from text most students at the university level miss between 60- 70% of the key points. Sixty one percent of students find it difficult to sequence ideas effectively to make coherent sense and more than half of all students report that their notes are disorganised.

At the secondary school level some teachers try to compensate for these note-making skill deficiencies by handing out copies of all the notes students need, or by developing notes where a child just has to fill in a key word, or by requiring children to copy notes directly from a textbook. Unfortunately, teaching strategies such as these do not give students the practice they need in creating good notes for themselves. Learning how to simultaneously observe, listen and create clear, concise, coherent notes is a key learning skill requiring initial training and lots of practice in order to perfect it.

Even if teachers do provide all the written material, most students study for tests purely by rereading those notes and most of them do all that rereading the day before the test. Of students who do try to actively process the information they need, most copy out their notes word-for-word, as very few have any effective summerising strategies.

I think good note-making, as I have described it, is an essential skill for all school students, in all countries. I also think it is only one of a collection of core generic learning skills that need to be taught to all students everywhere. Unfortunately it is a minority of teachers who believe teaching children how to learn needs to be a priority in their education and a minority of schools that have their own generic learning skills programme. I believe it should be compulsory.

Critical thinking	Critiquing texts, media, ideas and issues
Creativity and Innovation	Developing unique technologies and ideas
Collaboration	Cooperating with others
Communication	Transferring ideas and information through both word based and non-word based means
Time Management	Managing time and tasks
Information Literacy	Creating, finding, interpreting and judging information
Media Literacy	Interacting with, comparing and contrasting different media representations of information

So what are the most important learning skills, and how can those be broken down into simple strategies and techniques of effective learning?

There are three key sets of skills that are intrinsic to the learning process. They are the cognitive, the affective and the metacognitive.

i) Cognitive skills

Cognitive skills are those involved primarily in the use and practice of information processing and information retrieval strategies. The specific cognitive skills which have been shown in the literature to bring about the most significant improvements in learning for students at school are:

▫ Making effective notes – both in the classroom situation and at home during study

▫ Key word summarising – mind mapping, spider diagrams

▫ Using structural writing planners – for writing different types of essays and reports, also for creating poetry, for analysing novels, for all writing tasks

▫ Time management – goal setting, timetabling study time for assignments, tests, exams

▫ Memory techniques – mnemonics, multi-sensory techniques, visualisation, review

▫ Understanding their own learning preferences – mental representation, environmental and experiential preferences

▫ Self-assessment – learning to accurately judge and critique their own work

Cognitive skills are probably the easiest of the three skill sets for children to learn for themselves and it is for that purpose that I wrote my other book – *The Art of Learning for Students: Exam Confidence* (available on my website www.taolearn.com). This book is designed as a resource for students who need to learn the specific skills needed to study effectively and pass exams. This book is designed to be used by students themselves as a self-teaching resource but can also be used by teachers or parents to help guide the children in their care.

There are of course many more cognitive skills needed for successful learning than just those needed for study and exams and I hope to be producing more resources for children in the near future.

The framework of cognitive skills that I believe are most significant for any child's learning is on the facing page:

"Success is achieved by developing our strengths, not by eliminating our weaknesses."

Theodore Rubin

ii) Affective skills

In addition to the cognitive skills mentioned above it is also advantageous for students to learn techniques and strategies that enable them to gain some control over their emotional state, their motivation and what we tend to call attitude. These are the skills that students need to build resilience, to deal effectively with setbacks and difficulties, to learn how to self-motivate, manage emotional upsets, develop mindfulness and persevere.

While some people will think of attitude as an innate factor of personality there is good evidence to suggest that any attitude is often the manifestation of an habitual response to a situation that have been learned over a lifetime. Any habit that has been learned can be unlearned and relearned in a more effective way through strategies like attribution retraining, mentioned before. Teaching children how to deliberately change what they attribute as the cause of their learning failure or poor performance (eg. from a lack of ability to a lack of effort) has brought about improvements in reading persistence and comprehension, mathematics scores, achievement motivation and self esteem.

A basic framework of affective skills could include:

- self-compassion
- empathy
- self-motivation
- perseverance and persistence
- emotional management
- resilience
- mindfulness
- courage

One example of affective skill development which is happening in some schools right now is Mindfulness training. Through this training, by learning how to reduce exam anxiety, overcome distractions and increase their concentration and focus students have significantly improved their academic performance.

Some affective skills can be directly taught. In my own courses we deliberately put students into situations where they are challenged to learn new things and then teach them attribution retraining strategies to help them unlearn unsuccessful mental habits and start to build new more successful habits of mind.

"Never bend your head, always hold it high - look the world straight in the face."

Helen Keller

Other affective skills are best taught by parents. You can help your children to start to notice the unique character of their own mental state in moments when they are naturally experiencing affective skills like:

□   empathy and sympathy
□   compassion
□   persistence and perseverance
□   focus and concentration
□   resilience
□   self-motivation
□   courage

and at times when they find they are able to:

□   overcome distractions
□   concentrate
□   reduce anxieties
□   delay gratification
□   manage self-talk

All children experience these states of mind at different times, the thing is to get them to notice their own automatic, naturally occurring mental strategies in those situations and then to help them learn how to implement those strategies in a more deliberate manner when they need to. Parents can often assist with this process by helping their children to notice moments when they are demonstrating the most useful affective skills and just gently asking them to think about how they do that. If they are persisting and persevering to completion with something that they love then that proves that they can do it. They then have to learn how to duplicate that same mental state deliberately when they are engaged with something that they don't enjoy so much – like schoolwork. All affective skills manifest as states of mind.

Step 1: decide which affective skill you are going to focus on at home (perseverance, concentration, resilience etc.) and for how long (one at a time, for days, weeks, months etc.)

Step 2: develop a clear definition of the skill and create practical examples of a Beginner and a Master in that skill – define examples of the best and worst performance of that skill

Step 3: get your child to think of a time from their own life when they were demonstrating the particular skill

"Life can best be understood backward but we have to live it forward. This means continually stepping into uncertainty."

Charles Handy

Step 4: get them to close their eyes and remember that time as clearly as possible, to focus on what they could see, what they could hear, what they were saying to themselves, how it felt, any relevant sensations that were going on at the time and get them to think about any things they were noticing that they were particularly doing to generate that state of mind

Step 5: get them to open their eyes and write down as many of those things they remembered as possible

Step 6: create opportunities for your child to demonstrate or practice that particular skill and get them to try and duplicate the actions they wrote down as a deliberate strategy

Step 7: get them to add any new observations to their original description until they have a clear strategy they can practice whenever they need it.

I think Affective skill development is absolutely vital for all students to provide a solid platform upon which all achievement both academic and personal can grow. Just imagine if your children could, at will, switch on the mental resources they need to concentrate well, persevere and motivate themselves. Any goal would then be possible.

The frame work I have given you above is built on the inherent belief that all children know how to generate all these Affective states of mind already, it is just that maybe they haven't yet learned how to do that deliberately. The more you can help your children to notice when they do, the more they will learn how to do it for themselves when they need to.

iii) Metacognitive skills

Whether metacognition is a function, a skill set or simply an awareness is open to debate. However it is described, metacognition is the overarching function that enables all other learning skill improvement to take place. The metacognitive function is that part of our thinking that is always observing the results of our thinking and learning, looking to make changes and try out new ideas where necessary, implementing changes and reflecting on the results.

Of the three skills sets it is the metacognitive which acts as the executive thinking skill through which the greatest improvements in learning success can come.

The metacognitve function can be divided into two aspects

- metacognitive knowledge – the learner's awareness and knowledge of their own learning and thinking processes and
- metacognitive performance – the learner's skill in using that knowledge to make sustainable changes which improve the effectiveness and efficiency of their own learning

One new thing that I learned recently was...	Where was I?	What time of day was it?	How was I being taught pictures, diagrams, listening, discussing, hands-on, other activity...?	What did I do with the information – write notes, solve problems, draw diagrams ...	Who helped me to understand?

And also:

Metacognitive activities for regulating and overseeing learning include:

i)   planning: goal setting, choosing strategies, scheduling time and resources

ii) monitoring: checking progress, reviewing, rescheduling and evaluating outcomes: in both process and content

One area where parents sometimes work against the development of a child's metacognitive skills is by doing all the management of their learning for them. Parents often feel the need to do so because their children seem to be very disorganised and there is just so much to keep track of. Unfortunately by doing this they are depriving their children of a great opportunity to learn how to self-manage their own learning.

Of course at a young age all children need their parents to help with time management and organisation, but a smart parent always involves the child in the process as well to help them learn how to do it for themselves.

Of the three types of skills it is the metacognitve skill that is the most important one to focus on first. In practice, metacognition means children thinking about their thinking, noticing what they are doing with the information they are receiving in class, stepping outside what they are learning and looking at how they are learning. For parents this means first helping your children to notice their own thinking and learning processes, and then helping them learn to evaluate their processes from the point of view of effectiveness.

a)   Metacognitive Knowledge - Learning Logs

The best way for any child to work out how they learn most effectively is to start to notice when they do. Every child can think of some lessons at school that really worked for them and some lessons that didn't. To work out how they learn best they need to start thinking about what the conditions are that seem to predispose them to learn well. What goes with good learning for them? Is it a particular way in which they received the information – how it was presented? Was it what they then did with the information – how they processed it? Was it a particular resource? Was it a particular time of day?

The following exercise can be done at regular intervals with children and will help them start to think more metacognitively. Using first the table on the facing page, get your child to describe as best they can one or two instances from recent memory when they learned well. They can fill in what they learned, where they were and roughly what time of day it was. And then they need to remember how they were being taught (if there was a teacher present), what they did with this information and whether anyone else helped them to learn well.

Each instance of effective learning could be in the classroom or it could be in private or independent study, it could be on the sports field or when they are pursuing their interests. The point of the exercise is to build up the metacognitive habit of noticing learning and teaching strategies while they are happening.

One time recently that I noticed that I wasn't learning well was...	Where was I?	What time of day was it?	How was I being taught- pictures, diagrams, listening, discussing, hands-on, other activity...?	What did I do with the information – write notes, solve problems, draw diagrams ...	I found it difficult to learn because...?

Having completed that exercise children can them use the table from this page to do a similar analysis of one or two moments recently when they did not learn well. When a teacher or coach was trying to teach them something but when the learning just didn't stick.

If these exercises are completed regularly then it won't take long to build up enough data for the student to start to draw some tentative conclusions about the conditions that appear to help them learn well.

The conditions particular to their own way of learning can then be assembled into a learning strategy library which is simply a record of successful strategies employed. This can be utilised when that student is engaged in doing their homework or studying for tests and exams.

Analysis of learning experiences will not only yield information on strengths, it will also provide data on weaknesses. It can be useful for the student to notice the times when they tend to drift off and the particular teaching methods being employed when their attention wanders. Once they start to notice these times, they can then take on the challenge of learning how to focus and concentrate more deliberately, and can test themselves with those instances which they know have not worked for them in the past. Learning how to overcome your natural tendencies to distraction is a great achievement. Learning how to deliberately apply the most effective strategies for learning at all times when you need to is the number one skill for the successful student. Learning well when the subject matter is engaging or the teacher is enthusiastic is easy, it is learning well even when the conditions are completely against you that marks out the top student.

I am not a great fan of using questionnaire based learning styles models as a diagnostic tool to change and improve a child's strategies of learning. To paraphrase author Ian Stewart "if our brain was simple enough for us to understand we would be too simple to understand it." Any questionnaire will only, at best, give a brief view of thinking at that particular moment and can never reveal the full depth and complexity of an individual's own way of learning. The best way to help a child find out how they learn well is to help them to notice moments when they do.

This is their own way of learning at work.

"I hated every minute of training, but I said, 'Don't quit. Suffer now and live the rest of your life as a champion."

Muhammad Ali

b)   Metacognitive Performance

Once your child has started to become more aware of the effect of different learning strategies on the effectiveness of their own learning they can build on that awareness through focusing on metacognitive performance.

First it is important to be clear about how improvements in learning effectiveness are going to be measured. For this process I suggest students adopt a three aspect reflection strategy focused on:

▫ **Content** – reviewing the subject matter explored and learned at school from the point of view of understanding, application and retention of content

▫ **Skills** – reviewing ongoing improvements in proficiency in the skills of effective learning

▫ **Strategy Use** – reviewing progress in the implementation of different learning strategies, skills and techniques and the impact of these strategies on learning success

i)   Reflection on Content and Understanding — Homework

All too often I see homework given out by teachers that either covers material that was inadequately processed in class or is make-work, that which asks students to redo work they have understood well already. I think there is only one viable justification for homework and that is to consolidate the learning achieved during that day at school. This can be done through a process of reviewing understandings, finding any problems, creating questions and assimilating content into long term memory by making summaries of key points.

Each night, make sure your children:

i)   read through all the notes they took that day at school, pull out the key ideas covered and make them into a summary of key points

ii)   check their understanding of all the information covered that day and for any points not understood and formulate written questions along the lines of:

▫ What I don't understand yet is ....?

▫ How do you get from .... to.................?

▫ How do I ....?

▫ What I have done so far is .... but what do I have to do to ....?

▫ What I need to know is ....

▫ The bit that I just don't get is ....

▫ What do you mean when you say ....?

These questions can then be given to the appropriate teachers or can be addressed by parents or private tutors.

"If we did all the things we are capable of, we would literally astound ourselves."

Thomas A. Edison

I am a great advocate of homework but only homework which seeks to review and check understandings gained during the day at school.

ii) Reflection on Learning Skill Proficiency — Self - Assessment

This is the step that is easiest to avoid but is also the step that can make the biggest difference.

In this step the student tries to get very clear data on all the conditions pertaining to their own experience of learning effectively and efficiently, and then uses that data to modify and continually improve all their school subject-based learning.

The two key aspects of reflection on process are skills and strategy use. On a regular basis children need to reflect on their proficiency in the skills of effective learning and on the efficacy of all the learning strategies they have been exposed to.

You and your children together can develop a personalised list of the skills you think would be most useful for them to practice in order to perform well at school. Some of those that I have highlighted so far include the cognitive skills of:

- making effective notes
- key word summarising,
- time management
- memory techniques

and the affective skills:

- self-motivation
- perseverance and persistence
- concentration and focus
- resilience
- mindfulness

The details of how to teach and learn each of the first group of skills are covered in my self-teaching book: *The Art of Learning for Students – Exam Confidence*. For the second group, the affective skills, I hope I have given you one effective process you can use to focus on and develop these skills within your children. It is also possible to put all these skills together into one experiential development programme as we try to do on our courses and I am sure there are professionals in your part of the world who can provide this service as well.

"Your present circumstances
don't determine where you can
go; they merely determine where
you start."

Nido Qubein

The metacognitive part of learning skill development is not in the teaching or learning of the skills themselves, it is in helping your children to notice their own improvement in these skills as they learn more and become more confident.

If you are still familiarising yourself with this idea, why not talk it over with your child and see if you can reach agreement about which skill to focus on first. Just take one skill to begin with eg. concentration. Next, as we did with the affective skills training, reach agreement with your child on a clear definition of the skill and examples of the best and worst performance, examples of a Beginner and a Master in that skill –

Eg.   **Beginner** – can keep mind focused on one task for 10 seconds

    Master – can keep mind focused on one task for one hour

Then try to come up with some intermediate standards

Eg.   **Beginner** – can keep mind focused on one task for 10 seconds

    Learner – can keep mind focused on one task for 1 minute

    Apprentice – can keep mind focused on one task for 10 minutes

    Ace – can keep mind focused on one task for 30 minutes

    Master – can keep mind focused on one task for one hour

Make up your own, but get agreement on what the standards are and then make up some sort of chart which shows the levels and your definitions.

Then ask your child to self-assess their own proficiency in this skill and make a mark on the chart. Do not interfere with their self assessment. This is the metacognitive moment, let them put themselves where they will. The important thing for parents to do is everything and anything that helps them to move up that scale in all the skills they need to do well at school. If, by the time your child leaves school, they are at **Master** level in all the most important learning skills then I think they will have everything they need to be successful in the world of today and in the world of the future.

iii)   Reflection on Learning Strategies - Multi-Sensory Learning

As I have said before I am not a great fan of learning styles models especially those that use a questionnaire approach to diagnose a student's supposed best way of learning. I think that convincing someone that they are a visual or auditory learner is of no use if it puts that person in a box. The aim of becoming a great learner is to break out of the box and learn how to learn from any person, in any style, at any time, in any place, through any media. I find most learning styles models to be individually self-limiting and of very little use.

"Happiness does not come from doing easy work but from the afterglow of satisfaction that comes after the achievement of a difficult task that demanded our best."

Theodore Isaac Rubin

What I would suggest though is that characterising a child's best way of learning through their own experience can have great value and can be a very useful tool in helping children to become more effective learners. As long as you and your children both realise that learning well requires the combination of many factors- skills, emotions, abilities, attitudes, opportunities, perceptions, interpretations, distractions and environmental factors and no simple model will give you all the answers.

One place to obtain data is from the learning logs mentioned previously. If they are used frequently, maybe once a week or once a fortnight, then it doesn't take long to build up data. This will provide you with information on both moments when learning happened well and moments when it didn't. These logs only focus on teaching/learning moments but that data can tell a child a lot about themselves. The thing for parents to watch out for are any strategies that children can identify that seem to work well for them.

If your child is saying they didn't learn well because they don't like the teacher or the teacher doesn't like them, that is not a strategy, that is an emotional response. A strategy that might help in such a situation could be something like:

"How do I get myself to concentrate at times when I don't really feel like it? How do I do that?"

"Can I think of a time when I focused well even though I was bored or unhappy? How did I do that?"

Or more specifically something like "When we watch video in class I tend to get very sleepy but when we discuss it afterwards in groups I am wide awake. So it appears to me that I seem to learn best when ...."

Once a student has built up a library of strategies they can try deliberately using them where and when they need them – this is the essence of metacognitive performance.

If your child doesn't really understand the concept of strategies of learning or just can't think of any, then the best place to find new strategies is on the internet. Specifically in one of the more than one hundred school subject based websites that have appeared on the internet in the last five years.

There are many websites for each subject and also many websites that cover a multitude of subjects. There are websites which specialise in video presentations, those that have great spoken voice and those that offer games to play. All sensory means of processing information are available on the internet on these sites and any child can try learning on several sites and find out for themselves which strategies, techniques and media seem to work best for them.

"The real voyage of discovery consists not in seeking new landscapes, but in having new eyes."

Marcel Proust

If this is all a bit new for you I have some suggestions:

www.taolearn.com/students.php

This my site with many tips for students and links to many free websites to help with study. I have grouped the links by subject and described their level and suitability for specific qualifications.

www.topmarks.co.uk

This is an excellent search engine for school subject-based websites. You select the subject you want at the level you want and it brings up a big list of the suitable websites. You need to be familiar with British level indicators:

Age Level:

Early Years	=	less than 5 yrs old
Key Stage 1	=	5 – 7
Key Stage 2	=	7 – 11
Key Stage 3	=	11 – 14
Key Stage 4	=	14 – 16
Advanced	=	16 – 18
Higher Ed	=	over 18

Just a few examples of good school subject-based websites students have recommended to me are:

khanacademy.org- really clear clips explaining every part of most subjects

brightstorm.com- great videos and much more in Maths, Science and (American) English

getrevising.co.uk/resources- all subjects at all levels, great new shared resources arriving from other students daily

studyblue.com/notes/high-schools/- make and share online flashcards, quizzes and notes, study on-line and on your phone

johndclare.net and **spartacus.schoolnet.co.uk** – History sites, all countries, all ages

s-cool.co.uk and **bbc.co.uk/schools/gcsebitesize/**- good resources for all subjects

quizlet.com and **easynotecards.com/index**- flash card makers for most subjects

studyblue.com- notes, flashcards, games in every subject, share resources

sparknotes.com/- English Literature – analysis of characters, themes, plots, of books, plays, Shakespeare

swipestudy.com- free flashcard memory study games for most subjects – sent to your phone!

"The great thing in this world is not so much where we are, but in what direction we are moving."

Oliver Wendell Holmes

freeology.com- downloadable information organizers to help you write every type of essay or report

xtremepapers.com and freeexampapers.com- past exam papers in most educational systems

codecademy.com/#!/exercises/0 – learn to write the code you need to design websites, games and apps

I think every student needs to have at least one website that they are familiar with for every subject. And have them saved as favourites on their computer so they can always find them when they need them to answer any question they have in that subject. The thing about this generation of students that makes them different from all the generations of students before them is the internet. Your children are the very first digital age, they have grown up immersed in the internet but not many of them have yet learned how to use it effectively for study.

When I went to school, if you didn't understand something the way the teacher taught it or the way it was represented in the text book you were stuck. These days students always have another place to go to find a different way of helping them to understand any topic.

Once a student has established one website that works for them in every subject they may notice by reflection that the websites they find best for them all present information in a certain way – mostly videos, podcasts, flashcard games etc. This once again is a metacognitive moment, when a child starts to notice their own best ways of learning, from their own experience.

"Nothing in the world can take the place of perseverance, talent will not; genius will not; education will not; persistence and determination alone are omnipotent"

Calvin Coolidge

10. Action – Only One Way To Fail Well

Back in 2005, at the ripe old age of 50, I began studying for my Masters degree in Education. My topic was resilience in high ability children and I was studying a group of about 100 students at a local high school.

The group included students of all grades, from 13–18 years old. My investigation was into any links between their resilience and their academic performance.

These students were the top performers at this school at every level from Year 9 (13 year olds) to Year 13 (18 year olds). All bright, interesting and interested and a pleasure to work with and I was trying to find a link between their resilience and their academic performance.

It was this work that led me to most of the research I have mentioned in this book and also led me to develop my Gnostates analysis mentioned earlier.

I ran them all through my Gnostates analysis and discovered that all the students reported an internal LOC – to different degrees but none demonstrated an external LOC at all. I was puzzled at first but reasoned that as all the students in the study were selected from the highest ability students in the school it was reasonable to assume that to get to that position they would have to have learned to internalise some control in order to achieve at the highest level already. The students did however show great differences in orientations towards optimistic or pessimistic thinking. These two results placed all of these students in the two quadrants of Stoic and Resilient and none at all in either the Hopeful or Vulnerable quadrants.

Half way through my study all of my student group sat an end-of-year academic exam. Although all my students had great ability, somewhat surprisingly they did not all pass their exams well. Some of them passed brilliantly getting the highest possible results in some cases. Others did reasonably well considering their abilities but some of them did very badly either failing completely or just scraping by with the minimum possible grade (these I classified into the *High Achiever, Achiever* and *Underachiever* groups).

My next discovery was that with these students there was no connection at all between their academic success and their resilience. Students from all three groups, *High Achievers, Achievers* and *Underachievers*, were found spread across both the Resilient and the Stoic quadrants. Those who were demonstrably more resilient were no more likely to succeed or fail academically than those who were demonstrating more helplessness. This was something of a bombshell because it ran counter to established resilience research which in most cases suggested a direct correlation between resilience and academic achievement. The only exception to the rule I found in work by Delisle et al. who suggested that for some students their most resilient response under academic pressure was simply to opt out. When faced with an unstimulating and unchallenging curriculum

"I am not discouraged because every wrong attempt discarded is another step forward."

Thomas Edison

some high ability students, in order to preserve their own resilience and sense of self-worth, adopt a strategy of disengagement as their only honourable response by becoming what are called selective consumers.

I reasoned once again that as the students in my sample all were taken from the 'gifted' group maybe those that did poorly in their exams were actively choosing to do so and preserving their resilience by failing their exams.

If resilience was not the distinguishing factor between the highest and lowest achievers, my challenge was to try and discover what was.

To do this I then took the students from the *Achiever* group out of my analysis so that I could focus only on any significant differences between the students at the two ends of the achievement scale – the highest achieving students compared with the lowest achieving. I hoped that by eliminating the middle group I would make the differences between the extremes more explicit. I controlled the student achievement results for resilience and formed matched pairs of students with identical Gnostates ratings where one student in each pair was from the *High Achiever* group and one was from the *Underachiever* group. I then interviewed these students thoroughly and explored their differences.

Immediately some significant differences became clear. Across all pairs of students the practical strategies and internal characteristics of students who were *High Achievers* were noticeably different to those students who were in the *Underachievers* group. The *High Achievers* all demonstrated:

- involvement in extra-curricular activities
- intense interests or passions
- intellectual curiosity, academic engagement, a drive for understanding
- gaining enjoyment from significant challenge
- an active and clear goal focus
- using active strategies to learn from failure
- choosing to succeed

But it was around the concept of failure that I started to see the greatest differences.

I defined failure in this study as not reaching a personal goal. Setting a goal to be successful in some endeavour, to win a game, to make a product, to create something beautiful, to perform in a certain way and then to not achieve that goal.

Their responses were very revealing.

The *High Achievers* all reported actively applying long term effort-based strategies for achievement in all areas, whereas the *Underachievers* only reported applying effort in response to immediate deadlines.

Failing Well	Failing Badly

□ Acknowledging your failures
  - taking responsibility for your own actions
  - working out what you did wrong,
  - making changes
  - having another go
	□ Blaming the school or the 'system'
	□ Blaming other people
	□ Pretending you never have any failures
	□ Adding drama to failures to avoid dealing with them
	□ Avoiding any activity that could possibly result in failure
	□ Dropping any activity after the first failure
	□ Making the same mistake over and over
	□ Universalising failure

Similarly with procrastination, all interviewees reported procrastination to be a problem for them but whereas the *High Achievers* were actively taking steps to get on top of the problem, the *Underachievers* were succumbing to it and resorting to last minute urgency to get them through.

A high level of understanding and acceptance of failure was also strongly exhibited by the *High Achievers* in their interviews in contrast to the *Underachievers*. The *Underachievers* tended to deny that failure existed for them or took steps to avoid the possibility of failure in their lives. The one *Underachiever* who did acknowledge failure in his life reported feeling completely overwhelmed by what he saw as the total failure of everything in his life and so rendered himself completely helpless.

The responses to failure reported by the *Underachiever* group included:

- denying failure
- using ability attributions to explain any setbacks
- using no obvious strategies to reflect on and learn from mistakes
- eliminating any subject or task in which failure was experienced
- avoiding any situations where failure was possible
- believing that every personal action resulted in failure and it was impossible to change
- denying any successes
- focusing on own short-comings
- disengaging from the subject matter
- being content with underachievement.

In comparison the responses reported by the *High Achiever* group in dealing with failure were:

- using effort based attributions for any failure
- focusing on learning from mistakes
- being adaptable and achieving to the level of personal best
- using hard work, talent and organisation to limit failure
- being prepared to try new strategies and apply more effort
- establishing absolute control in important areas
- using precise goal focus and the application of organisation and effort to minimise failure
- viewing failure as temporary and specific
- taking responsibility for own actions in any failure situation.

Taking my lead from the information security industry I called one response to failure, ***failing well*** and the other response ***failing badly*** (see table on opposite page).

Failing Well	Failing Badly
Emotional reaction to failure is short lived and fuel for improved performance	Emotional reaction to failure is long lasting and debilitating
Expecting to experience some failure in new learning situations	Denying failure exists or believing that everything is failure
Using strategies to learn from failure	No strategies to learn from failure
Being adaptable and making changes where necessary	Focusing on own shortcomings, believing it is impossible to change
Using perseverance, organisation and effort to minimise the possibility of failure	Eliminating any subject or task in which failure is experienced
Establishing complete control in some areas	Avoiding situations where failure is possible
Viewing failure as temporary and specific eg. lack of effort	Viewing failure as pervasive and permanent eg. lack of intelligence
Taking responsibility for own actions in failure situations	Being content with underachievement

The most important thing to realise about this study was that the result I discovered was **100% significant. All** the students in the *High Achievers* group were demonstrating what I called failing well and **all** the students in the *Under Achievers* group were failing badly.

This was a very important finding for me because it appeared that I had identified one unique factor that consistently differentiated between those students who did well in their exams and those who did not.

Reaction to Failure

At this point in my study (2008) I hypothesised three possible ideas worth exploring:

1. That maybe there was a direct relationship between failing well and academic success for all students, not just for gifted students
2. That it seemed that there was only one way to fail well but there were many ways to fail badly
3. That the idea of failing well could create a new model of success. Previously, for any endeavour (goal, plan, task) there were only ever two possible outcomes – success or failure, but with this model there were always three possible outcomes: success, failing well and failing badly, and two of these were positive.

Which led me in turn to the idea that maybe there was a causal relationship between failing well and academic success. That learning to fail well might actually produce academic success.

Then I set out to see if I was right.

The Confirmation

For the last six years I have worked with many thousands of students, their parents and teachers in 14 different countries testing out this model and the results appear to be consistent across the world:

▫ Students who *fail well* do better, much better, than students who fail badly.
▫ Teachers who *fail well* do better.
▫ Parents who *fail well* do better.

The key to *failing well* seems to be in the reprocessing of failure and the best way to teach your children how to fail well is to model the process yourself.

Remember that my definition of failure is simply *not reaching a personal goal*.

"If at first you don't succeed, make sure you fail well."

Lance King

In that situation I suggest that both you and your children try following these steps:

1. Admit every failure – immediately
2. Get over your emotional attachment to the word failure. Failure is just feedback. Feedback on what you aren't doing right yet
3. Take responsibility for your own actions in not achieving that goal
4. Make changes
5. Have another go

Take a school situation as a simple example- imagine your child has just sat a Maths test with ten questions and they have got seven out of ten correct.

What do they do with the three out of ten they got wrong?

This is the crucial test.

Children that practice *failing well* will look at the seven out of ten they got right and feel OK about that, they passed. And then they will look at the three out of ten they got wrong and ask why? Then they will analyse each question, work out exactly what they did wrong, make corrections and make sure they know how to get the correct answer. Then they will do a couple more problems similar to each one of the ones they got wrong until they are confident they have nailed them all. Then they will put the whole test behind them.

Children that practice *failing badly* will look at the seven out of ten questions they got right and feel OK about that, they passed. Then they will put the whole test behind them.

This is a simple difference but a very significant one.

To sum up my failing well model:

The secret for parents in achieving success with my failing well model seems to lie in two significant areas where we need to help our children to:

1. Managing the emotional response to failure, and
2. Taking action to re-process the failure to turn failure into a learning experience.

This means that parents can help children to deal with any failure by always making sure they have another go, whatever the failure situation is, but making sure they change something first.

"It's fine to celebrate success but it is more important to heed the lessons of failure."

Bill Gates

Learn How to Fail Well

The first step, I think, is to reframe the word failure and define it as simply not reaching a goal you set for yourself. As parents if we specify failure in this way then we can help our children to understand that failure is just feedback. What failure is doing for you is giving you great information on what you aren't doing right, yet. Failure is a necessary part of growth, learning and achieving goals.

Unfortunately we often attach a lot of emotional baggage to the word failure, which I think comes about through treating failure as a condition rather than an action. I don't believe that a person can ever be a failure but the things they do can often fail. To help with this, when I am working with children I like to use the slogan on the facing page.

Next, as parents I think we have to model failing well. Any time we do not achieve a goal we set for ourselves we need to admit that as a failure immediately, take responsibility for our own actions in not achieving that goal, make changes and have another go.

Then we need to explicitly teach our children how to fail well. This is where the rubber meets the road, so to speak. Learning to fail well requires taking action. It is not simply a way of thinking, it is a habit, instilled by experience. The trick is to have a good process to follow.

The process I use is:

You could explain it to your child like this:

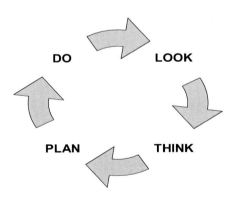

All through your life you are going to take action – that's the **DO Step.** Now imagine for a moment that you have done that, taken action, put planning and effort into something, and further imagine that it hasn't worked out well. Maybe you failed a test or an exam, or got a poor mark for an assignment, or you tried out for a certain sports team or theatre production and they didn't pick you, or maybe you didn't get a job you interviewed for, or a relationship or a business idea failed.

What do you do next, after you have achieved some emotional distance from the event? The least productive things you can do are blame someone else or try to forget about it. The best thing you can do is to move to the **LOOK Step** and describe what actually happened. In detail, step by step, before, through and after the event. Preferably written down, sticking absolutely to the facts leaving opinion and blame aside.

"Success - it is focusing the full power of all that you are on what you have a burning desire to achieve."

Wilfred A Peterson

Once the analysis is completed you can move to the **THINK Step** where, looking back at your description of what happened, you take responsibility for your own actions. All your own actions. And looking at your part in the event ask yourself two questions – "looking back:

1. The things I did that worked were......."
2. The things I did that didn't work were........"

Then finally you move to the **PLAN Step.** Looking at your list of things you did last time that didn't work, make a commitment to change at least one of them next time.

And then always, always, always..... make a change and have another go.

This is the essence of failing well — making a change and have another go.

From now on every task, every goal, every performance has not two but three possible outcomes – *Success, Failing Well and Failing Badly,* and two of these are positive. By adopting this model you instantly increase the potential for a positive outcome by one third.

To sum up:

▫   Help your children to see any academic failure as a failure of process not of the individual and as an important step to success
▫   Teach the skill of failing well
▫   Always allow for the reprocessing of failure
▫   Celebrate learning from mistakes

I guess the hardest things for parents in implementing my model is allowing your children to fail. This is really difficult. If you see your child making a stupid mistake or a bad decision your natural instinct is to intervene, to stop them, to eliminate the possibility of their failing before it's too late. But of course by doing that you are robbing them of the chance to learn from their own failures, to improve on their own performance and to become comfortable in making their own decisions and taking all the consequences.

In my household I like to think that one of our highest ethical practices was enabling our children to make their own mistakes, experience the consequences, make changes and have another go. Criticism of failure only produces children who are afraid of failing, scared of taking any chances or trying anything new and ultimately children who are paralysed into inaction.

Similarly with praise. The greatest praise, I think, should be reserved for times when someone learns from their mistakes, makes changes, goes through the experience again and produces an improved result. That is worth celebrating!

	Resilient high achieving self-regulated learners	Other students
Goals	Set learning goals – learn in order to understand	Set performance goals – learn in order to get the best grade
Tasks	Take on new tasks to test themselves, to work toward mastery	Take on new tasks to gain approval or avoid disapproval
Challenge	Actively seek out new challenges	Avoid all new challenges
To achieve success	Believe effort is more important than ability	Believe ability is more important than effort
Reaction to failure	Fail Well - take responsibility, focus on the process, find the problem, change the process, have another go	Fail Badly - take no responsibility, blame others, repeat the same process or do even less, give up
Reaction to Success	Attribute to self	Attribute to others
View of intelligence	Believe intelligence is flexible, can be developed and increased	Believe intelligence is fixed, unalterable with a definite limit
Performance	High achievers	Under achievers
Locus of Control	Internal	External
Future Expectations	Optimistic	Pessimistic

Self-Regulated Learners

If the aim of a school based education is to produce brilliant learners then I think I have discovered that the practice of failing well is the essential and necessary condition for the development of the resilient self-regulated learner. The self-regulated learners are those students who can learn for themselves, who have all the skills, aptitudes and attitudes they need, who are never put off by setbacks and who find learning itself to be fascinating whatever the subject. These students are the true self-managed, self-directed, self-motivated, autonomous, independent, lifelong learners.

These students employ a metacognitive process, as described previously, not only to monitor effective cognitive strategies for learning but also to monitor and regulate their emotional or affective responses in learning situations. They treat learning as a process requiring many different techniques and strategies depending on the subject and the context. They actively seek out options for every stage of the learning process, they try out different things and they notice what works and what doesn't.

To do this they are consciously engaged during study and learning with both their subject matter and the processes they are using to learn that subject matter. They view any learning failure as a failure of process rather than a failure of themselves. If they fail to achieve the learning goal they want, they find better processes and apply them, they reflect on the results and they continually improve the success of their learning efforts. They tend to focus on effort rather than ability, on learning for understanding rather than grades and they maintain a belief in the malleability of their own intelligence. They deliberately use delayed gratification and positive self-talk to generate self-motivation, they exhibit good impulse control, and in order to improve performance and learning, often use attention focusing tactics to screen out distractions and improve concentration.

Students who employ self-regulated, self-determined approaches to learning not only achieve higher levels of academic achievement than those that don't, they also experience a sense of personal satisfaction in their work and are more inclined to make adaptive changes to enhance future performance. Students that experience a greater sense of competence and self-direction in their daily learning are more likely to persist with difficult learning tasks and experience an enhanced sense of personal well-being and satisfaction upon completing those tasks.

These students are easy to identify in any class because they are diligent, hard-working and seem to really enjoy learning. With these students it is often difficult to separate out their natural talent from their dedicated application as they usually take out the top grades at school. They often get categorised as *gifted* and they may well be but their most important talent is the self-regulation of their own learning.

They know how to do it for themselves!